THE HUMAN RIGHTS BOOK

Also by Milton Meltzer

The
Human
Rights
Book

MILTON MELTZER

FARRAR, STRAUS, GIROUX • NEW YORK

Designed by Betty Crumley
Library of Congress Cataloging in Publication Data
Meltzer, Milton.
The human rights book.
Bibliography: p.
Includes index.
SUMMARY: Discusses the evolution of a concept of
human rights, how these rights are defined and
interpreted throughout the world, to what degree they
are observed or violated, and the international
institutions and agencies responsible for gaining and
maintaining these rights for individuals.
1. Civil rights—Juvenile literature. [1. Civil
rights] I. Title.
JC571.M398   1979   323.4   79–13017

Acknowledgment is made for permission to quote from the following works: *The Crowned Cannibals: Writing on Repression in Iran,* by Reza Baraheni, by permission of Random House, Inc., Copyright © 1976, 1977 by Reza Baraheni; interview with Mario Vargas Llosa, April 9, 1978, and statement by Mihajlo Mihajlov, April 9, 1978, reprinted by permission of *The New York Times,* Copyright © 1978 by The New York Times Company; excerpt from essay by Jan Kott in *The New York Review of Books,* August 17, 1978, reprinted with permission from *The New York Review of Books,* Copyright © 1978, Nyrev, Inc.; passage from "Human Rights, International Relations Theory and Regime Change," by Laurie S. Wiseberg, by permission of Laurie S. Wiseberg; excerpt from "Freedom Appeal," by Arthur Miller, 1978 PEN Newsletter, Issue 21, courtesy PEN American Center.

For Jeanette *and* William Herrick

CONTENTS

Where, after all, do universal human rights begin? In small places, close to home—so close and so small that they cannot be seen on any maps of the world. Yet they *are* the world of the individual person; the neighborhood he lives in; the school or college he attends; the factory, farm or office where he works. Such are the places where every man, woman and child seeks equal justice, equal opportunity, equal dignity with discrimination. Unless these rights have meaning there, they have little meaning anywhere. Without concerned citizen action to uphold them close to home, we shall look in vain for progress in the larger world.

Eleanor Roosevelt, *The Great Question*, United Nations, 1958

1

The Politics of Torment

Kidnapped, in bright afternoon, from the middle of the street.

They took him to his home, tore the place apart in their search for evidence, then hustled him off, blindfolded, to a building in the center of the city.

That night they interrogated him: name? married? children? brothers? sisters?

And then the charge—a crime against the state.

He denied he had committed that crime, or any other crime.

They had him sign a paper, and took him to a cell.

The next day it began:

I am beaten by the head torturer. My beard is pulled out with a pair of surgical scissors. I am given seventy-five blows on the soles of my feet with a plaited wire whip; one of my fingers is broken; I am threatened with the rape of my wife and daughter; then a pistol is held to my head at the temple by another torturer and, in fact, I hear it fired. I faint. When I open my eyes, I am being carried downstairs on the back of the soldier who tied my feet to the iron bed in the torture chamber and was introduced to me as the potential rapist of my wife and daughter.

As soon as the guard sets me down, one of the four civilians who were whipping me in the torture chamber appears and orders me to get up and stamp my feet on the ground.

I get up but fall down. There is blood all over my feet, and they are already as thick as two heavy mud bricks. The man wields his long wire whip in a circle around my head.

"Get up, you son of a bitch, and stamp your feet on the floor!"

I get up and start stamping my miserable feet on the floor. I look like a huge circus bear dancing heavily with a bleeding hemorrhoid. The whipper moves around me like a circus animal trainer. Then he tells me to sit down on the floor. He himself sits behind a desk.

I cannot put my feet on the floor. I try to examine my position, but my mind is fuzzy. The torture chamber is a nightmare from which I will never wake up. Who are these people? Why are they doing this to us? There are screams all over the place. Are they real or artificial? Are they genuine or recordings from past events?

Days later, after repeated interrogation, and his repeated refusal to admit to some undescribed political crime:

I am lying on the tiles of the floor with my bowl of food beside me. It is rice, with some kind of ugly-looking juice in it. I have so many pains, I don't know which one to think about first. I look at my feet. I can hardly recognize them. They are red and blue, and swollen, and they look very awkward with their stupid, obscene, protruding obesity . . .

Lying there on the floor, I know that I am alone and that I am the only person who can defend himself in this hell. The world outside is dead and buried; I have to do everything myself in this four-by-eight-foot hole. Everyone in the other cells is moaning, and I can hear the crying of men and women all the way up and down the corridor.

Are they really going to do what they told me they would do to my wife and daughter. Their lives don't belong to me. They haven't done anything against anyone. Why should they suffer?

The iron door of the ward opens, closes, opens and closes again. Thingified men and women crawl in the corridor. What time is it? How am I going to tell them that I believe in certain things for myself and that I don't have to believe in exactly the same things they believe in?

His thoughts wander. Has he been asleep and dreaming all these things? But there, squatting at the open cell door, is his interrogator:

He must have been looking at me for a long time. The guard is standing behind him. He is looking at me. All the other cells are silent. It must be midnight.

"Why you—a university professor, a well-known poet and a prominent journalist—should do something so that we will be forced to deal with you like some kind of criminal."

"But I haven't done anything."

He gets up and comes in, telling the guard to close the door and go away. Squatting again, he faces me.

"You have done something. Otherwise you wouldn't be here."

"There has been a misunderstanding. I haven't done anything."

"There is no misunderstanding. Everyone in this country, from the simple private in the army to the First Person of the Nation, knows that you are a traitor."

"Traitor to whom?"

He raises his hand and touches my cheeks, looking into my eyes. "You are a traitor. We have all the documents."

He slaps me on the face as hard as he can. I fall on the floor, and he kicks me and punches me with his fists. I start screaming. I know from the torture chamber that whenever I scream I feel some relief. The other prisoners are startled from their sleep and start screaming themselves. He goes on beating and cursing me.

I keep screaming.

He opens the door and shouts at the other prisoners, "You go to sleep, you bastards!"

They seem to know his voice. They fall silent. I crouch in a corner of the cell.

That is the voice of Reza Baraheni, a victim of his state, Iran. Poet, novelist, critic, translator, professor, he is one among the many millions unjustly deprived of their human rights in every part of the world, under every political system, from the furthest left to the furthest right.

Baraheni's country, Iran, has now seen the fall of its monarchy. Until the Shah's overthrow, an average of 1,500 people were arrested every month by the secret police. For one recent year the total number of political prisoners was reported at times to be anywhere from 25,000 to 100,000. Thousands of men and women were summarily executed by Iran in the last quarter of a century. Baraheni, imprisoned and tortured for 102 days, was released only under the pressure of public opinion. In response to an international cry of protest generated by several human rights organizations, he was let out of prison and exiled. Now he lives in the United States.

Reza Baraheni was lucky—if you can say that of a man

forced from his homeland. At least he survived and escaped his persecutors. But there are hundreds of thousands of others, prisoners of conscience, rotting in cells and concentration camps all over the world. Among them are not only artists like Baraheni but miners and ministers, peasants and physicians, labor organizers and scientists, teachers and students, men and women of every age and occupation. And children too, children imprisoned simply because they are born of parents the state wishes to silence or destroy.

In preparing for this book I read the daily press regularly and day after day clipped one, two, three, sometimes as many as half a dozen reports of people whose human rights were being violated in some corner of the globe. And this, I soon realized, was but a token of the reality. For every victim whose story surfaces in the press there are a great many anonymous others whose suffering is endured in the silent dark.

Why does the state strike at such people? Out of fear, always, a fear felt by those who control the government. Their power is threatened, they think, and they mean to crush anyone who questions their authority or actions. In the case of Reza Baraheni, he had written a book in which he protested against the oppression of the nationalities in Iran. There are several ethnic minorities but all were ordered to forget their own language and to read and write and speak only the official Persian. (The control extended even unto death. On the gravestone of his father, Baraheni was not permitted to carve his name in their Turkish tongue—only a number.) Baraheni spoke up, too, against the subjugation of women and the censorship of writers. Dissent in the one-man state of the Shah summoned up the torturers. No one is safe in a country where elementary democratic rights do not exist.

But the issue of human rights is not confined to the elimination of repression and torture. We think of these first because the violence they do to the human spirit and body touches us deeply and at once. And in America, and what we call "the West," there has for centuries been a great awareness of political, civil, and religious rights. We have been raised on the Constitution and the Bill of Rights. We know about them in our bones. But elsewhere in the world, other rights have come to have just as powerful a meaning. The right to fulfillment of such vital needs as food, shelter, health care, work, education—these are now among the universal human rights. They are at the core of the struggle for social and economic justice.

What gave rise to the idea of human rights? What does the world take them to mean? To what degree are they observed or violated, both here at home and abroad? In our foreign policy do we challenge or support repressive governments? To what international institutions and agencies can the peoples of the world look for support in fulfilling human rights?

And what, finally, can one person do who cares about human rights? Where can one turn for information and guidance? Where can one find neighbors to share in the effort to stem destructiveness and secure dignity, peace, and freedom?

2

To Be Human

To live and be free . . .

Almost no one contests these as the natural rights of all people.

It is the essence of what the world means by the term "human rights."

Yet progress to this understanding, surmounting ignorance and prejudice, has been slow. To trace in any detail the historic evolution of these ideas is beyond the scope of this book. But if we single out a few of the turning points, the reader will have a clearer view of human rights in today's world.

Let's stop for a moment at the word "human." What does being human mean? To be human is to be part of humanity—all human beings taken collectively, the human race, mankind. That concept is rather recent, say the cultural anthropologists. In some cultures the term "man" was confined to members of one's own tribe. Outsiders or strangers were not viewed as men. Such societies had few abstract concepts. Their members, centered on themselves, did not yet understand that they and strangers, too, were part of common humanity. The idea that all people are equal on the basis of their common human nature took a very long time to evolve. One place it arose was in ancient Greece, where philosophers gave it the name *humanitas.*

The concept of humanity is found, too, in the tradition of the Old and New Testaments. If man is fashioned in God's image, then man has an inner dignity and freedom, which should be respected no matter what particular political or social system he lives under.

Not until the seventeenth and eighteenth centuries did ideas of natural law and natural right give rise to a political concept of human rights. "We hold these truths to be self-evident, that all men . . . are endowed by their Creator with certain un- alienable rights . . ." So the thinking ran in the American colonies. The British king had no divine right to be supreme; it was the people who were sovereign, and any ruler should respect and guard their dignity. The state existed for them, not they for the state. The colonials who won their independence in the American Revolution asserted the right to take part in "ordaining the Constitution" under which they would live.

Out of this belief in popular sovereignty the Americans spun the first agreement on human rights: the Bill of Rights amend- ing the U.S. Constitution. It placed limitations on the arbitrary exercise of the government's power against the individual. The citizen was to be free from encroachments upon his rights by the state. The Bill of Rights began with the freedoms of the First Amendment—speech, press, religion—and went on to freedom from unreasonable search and seizure, the security of property, due process of law, the right to a fair trial and civilized punishment. In addition to particular rights protected against government invasion, the Bill of Rights reaffirmed other rights "retained by the People."

The Constitution of the United States ("We the people") as well as the early state constitutions, reflected these rights. So did the Declaration of the Rights of Man and of the Citizen, which came out of the French Revolution. Such compacts arrived at in the struggle for citizenship became the foundation of human rights. Most of the constitutions under which the nations of the world govern today bear the imprint of that origin. Even where the reality of rule may be despotic or totalitarian, the constitutions are liberally sprinkled with references to "the people."

When the Universal Declaration of Human Rights was adopted in 1948 by the General Assembly of the new United Nations, it was without dissent. (The Soviet bloc of nations, which abstained at the time, later accepted the Declaration.) In the decades since 1948, almost every new nation has joined in supporting the Universal Declaration.

So the *idea* of human rights is universally accepted. While political observers may insist that human rights in many places are only paper rights, still, no government today would declare it is opposed to human rights. There is some disagreement as to precisely which rights need emphasis, or which deserve priority, but national and international constitutions and institutions give at least lip service to them. The constitutions of both the Soviet Union and the People's Republic of China refer to them.

The socialist states have added another dimension to human rights. To them, the views of human rights in such countries as Great Britain and the United States appear to be too general and abstract. They think such definitions of human rights tend to conceal the true social and economic conditions, safeguarding the rights of only the privileged class. It is not that socialists challenge the need to protect human dignity; rather, that they want it made realizable by creating the social and economic conditions which would enable all people, especially the deprived, to exercise their human rights. This, they hold, is possible only in a socialist society. The rights of that collective, then, take priority over the rights of the private individual. They interpret human rights to mean, first of all, the right to adequate food, shelter, housing, education, work. And in the international documents these social and economic rights have now come to be included alongside political and civil rights.

Among the Third World nations, sometimes called the "developing nations," there is still another concept of human rights. Their priorities are somewhat different. Their attention is focused on the basic necessities of survival in the face of the famine which threatens so many of the less-developed countries. They are bent on abolishing the colonial structures left them when the imperial powers departed. They strive to overcome racial discrimination and to recover their cultural heritage. The rights of individuals, so prominent in the West, seem relatively less important to Third World nations facing the elemental challenge of survival. They place life-sustaining conditions for work and food at the head of human rights, together with the elimination of exploitation within their countries and by the powers beyond their borders.

In whatever way they differ, these concepts of human rights are not contradictory. They complement one another, they are interdependent. That relationship, however, is not always or easily seen. Sometimes, at international assemblies or in public debate, the nations holding varying concepts clash. Their common stake in protecting human rights does not prevent tense and angry dispute. (There will be more to say on this later.)

Many thinkers have tried to reconcile such differences by formulating a common core of human rights. The number of rights listed in the basic documents (see Appendix) is large. They overlap in part or can be combined in simpler and more compact form. But wherever such attempts have been made at finding common ground, they are instantly criticized for what they leave out or because they reflect the bias of the author's culture and traditions. Professor Charles Frankel of Columbia, a philosopher, recently insisted that if the world is really serious about human rights, it should keep the list of them brief and limited. His argument is interesting. A right, he says, "is something that must be delivered, short of the most extreme excusing conditions." For example, the right not to be forced to confess must be delivered by police. It makes sense to tell a policeman he has an obligation not to torture you in order to extract information or a confession. Presumably, he can desist from torturing.

But take the rights which proclaim everyone is entitled to as much education as he wants, and to a decent level of health as well. In many countries, Frankel points out, the economy is so poor that the government cannot possibly satisfy both rights at once. In such circumstances rights are only aspirations. The capacity to deliver is not there, which distorts the ordinary meaning of the term "right." ("It is also cruel and impolitic," he believes; "it turns loose aspirations that can't be fulfilled, it makes people more unhappy and frustrated than they would otherwise be.")

Frankel therefore suggests a group of rights that meet two

tests: first, that they are genuinely felt choices just about every-where; and second, that they are deliverable. His list is small: the right not to be physically abused, due process with respect to criminal questions, protection in one's religion or irreligion, and protection of the family and its privacy. These, no matter what the form of government or nature and condition of the economy, can and should be satisfied, he claims.

His list was, of course, challenged. One critic said it might do for American export, considering conditions in the world at large. But in American society, and in others at a comparable stage of development, a much longer list of human rights is desirable and achievable.

Trying to view the issue as objectively as possible, one can see that all human rights are bound up with one another. How can one cut them down, or separate them from each other?

One interesting attempt to find a common basis and a common goal for human rights was made during years of study and discussion under the auspices of the World Alliance of Reformed Churches. Out of a concern for the "humanity of persons" came this six-point ecumenical "Common Ground on Human Rights." It reads:

(a) There is a basic human right to life—inclusive of the en-tire question of survival, of the threats and violations resulting from unjust economic, social and political systems, and of the equality of life.
(b) There is a right to enjoy and to maintain cultural identity —which includes issues such as national self-determination, the rights of minorities, etc.
(c) There is a right to participate in the decision-making process within the community—which comprises the entire issue of effective democracy.

(d) There is a right to dissent—which prevents a community or a system from hardening into authoritarian immobility.

(e) There is a right to personal dignity—which implies, for example, the condemnation of all torture and of prolonged confinement without trial.

(f) There is a right freely to choose a faith and a religion— which encompasses the freedom, either alone or in community with others, in public or in private, to proclaim one's faith by the means of teaching, practice, worship, and ritual.

Although human rights have become front-page news only in the last few years, the struggle for them has been an enduring part of human history. There is hardly any political movement of modern times which does not bear upon the issue. In the broadest sense, is not any effort to better man's condition part of the struggle for human rights? The centuries-long fight to abolish slavery (it still goes on), labor's fight for the right to organize and to improve its working and living conditions, women's battle for equal rights, the liberation movements of the colonial countries, the International Red Cross movement for humane treatment of prisoners and the wounded in war—all these and many others are examples of action on behalf of human rights long before that term became popular.

Here in America the impression still exists, however, that internationalization of human rights is a radically new policy initiated by President Carter. That is due to the traditional notion that a country should mind its own business. The state has sovereignty over its own territory, which means that how it treats persons within its borders is its own affair. What happens to human rights elsewhere is the business of those other countries. Unless, that is, their freedom to do certain things is forbidden by international law. And in international law there are some ancient precedents for such interference. Take how a country treats an alien. Two thousand years ago if a government injured a citizen of Rome, it injured Rome. And if today an American visiting a foreign country is abused, the United States is concerned. Governments for a long time have been offended by mistreatment of their citizens abroad, and in this sense the security of those citizens had been widely recognized as a human right. International law made it legitimate for governments to protect their citizens living in foreign countries.

In the mid-nineteenth century a concern for humanitarianism led to diplomatic conferences in the laws of warfare, and these culminated in the Geneva Convention of 1864 on treatment of the wounded in wartime. When the Turks committed atrocities against the Armenians in the late 1800s, there were attempts by some nations to stop the slaughter. These were moves in the direction of protecting the human rights of individuals in other states—of foreign people. It was a significant departure from the old norm of "mind your own business." But these efforts were without plan or continuity. They occurred only when particularly outrageous events roused deep popular feeling and caused great publicity.

The idea of an international standard of justice developed slowly. There was no legal definition of what it meant. But the notion of some standard of treatment—of "fairness"—was there for governments to invoke in protection of their citizens residing as aliens in other countries. There was no suggestion that the standard applied to how governments treated their own citizens. (That was still *their* business.) Governments rarely protested domestic injustice somewhere else. One exception occurred when widespread pogroms against the Jews of

Czarist Russia roused horror in America, and the United States government tried diplomatic means to halt them. Or again with British action against Ireland. Both cases are examples of government intervention prodded by a domestic group— the Jewish Americans and the Irish Americans—with intense sympathy for victims in the countries of their origin.

Even earlier, however, governments acted on the principle that what some other nation did might be more than a matter of local concern. In the seventeenth century there were agreements between Catholic and Protestant rulers about the treatment of one another's religious minorities. And later similar agreements extended to ethnic minorities. By the early 1900s the bigger powers of Europe imposed minority treaties on the smaller powers for fear that violation of minority rights might lead to war.

When the League of Nations was formed at the close of the First World War, its covenant expressed a concern for human rights. Countries joining the League accepted the obligation to maintain fair and humane conditions of labor, and to secure the just treatment of the indigenous peoples in their colonies. The mandates system, established under the covenant, charged those powers with the responsibility for the well-being and development of the local population. It was often said that the controlling powers had no real concern for human rights: the mandate was only a mask behind which the former colonial peoples were exploited. Still, it meant that international documents gave at least elementary recognition to the principle of human rights. With slavery abolished by now in most countries, international agreement was also reached to outlaw slavery and the slave trade. Still another example of the internationalization of human rights.

Working people who in many countries had already built trade unions now forged international links to advance and protect their rights. The International Labor Organization, formed at this time, and many international conventions promoted basic standards for labor conditions and social welfare. This, too, helped make human rights a worldwide concern. Steadily the outlook changed; more and more nations came to accept the idea that they have a moral responsibility for their actions. Not only under treaty obligations, but as a simple matter of justice.

Around the world, then, people have shown in action that they care about human rights, that they want to reduce man's suffering and protect his dignity. But only recently has it become an issue at the top of the international political agenda. It was the Second World War and the Holocaust—Hitler's planned destruction of the Jews—which made human rights the concern of international law. The close connection between the Nazi government's murderous behavior toward a section of its own citizens and its aggression against other nations became clear to many. They saw respect for human rights was related to the maintenance of peace. Out of the experience of that war came the universal conviction that effective international protection of human rights was an essential condition of international peace and progress. Even while the war was being fought, that growing conviction was voiced in several ways.

One example was the Atlantic Charter of 1941. In it President Roosevelt of the United States and Prime Minister Churchill of Great Britain expressed the hope of seeing "established a peace which will afford to all nations the means of dwelling in safety within their own boundaries, and which will afford assurance that all the men in all the lands may live out their lives in freedom from fear and want." (Another forty-seven nations later endorsed the charter.)

Months later, in 1942, twenty-six nations then at war signed the Declaration of the United Nations. They agreed that "complete victory over their enemies is essential to defend life, liberty, independence and religious freedom, and to preserve human rights and justice in their own lands as well as in other lands."

In 1944, at Dumbarton Oaks, proposals were made to establish a general international organization to be called the United Nations. It would, among other things, "facilitate solutions of international economic, social and other humanitarian problems and promote respect for human rights and fundamental freedoms." Dumbarton led to the San Francisco Conference of 1945, where the United Nations Charter was prepared. It refers to human rights in its preamble and in six different articles. Through the preamble the peoples of the United Nations express determination "to reaffirm faith in fundamental human rights, in the dignity and worth of the human person, in the equal rights of men and women and of nations large and small." The words "promoting and encouraging respect for human rights" and "assisting in the realization of human rights and fundamental freedoms" appear, with certain variations, in Articles 1, 13, 55, 56, 62, and 76.

All members of the UN pledge themselves to take joint and separate action to achieve its purposes, among them "universal respect for, and observance of, human rights and fundamental freedoms for all without distinction as to race, sex, language, or religion."

The UN charged its Economic and Social Council with the

task of making recommendations promoting human rights and basic freedoms. To carry out that function, the council set up a Commission on Human Rights. One of America's delegates to the formative meetings of the UN was Eleanor Roosevelt, widow of the President. No one better personified respect for human dignity than Mrs. Roosevelt, and she was elected chairperson of the "nuclear" commission, whose job it was to draft an international bill of human rights.

In the early debates of the commission philosophic differences quickly became apparent. The Yugoslav representative pointed out that many of the proposals for a bill of human rights reflected the social and political ideas of the middle class and were now obsolete. In the modern world, he said, the social principle should have priority. It was impossible to consider individuals except collectively. The representative for Lebanon, a Christian humanist, replied that the "human person" is "prior" to any group to which he may belong, whether it be class, race, or nation. His "mind and conscience" were the "most sacred and inviolable things about him." The group "can be wrong, just as the human person can be; in any case it is only the human person who is competent to judge." Many entered both sides of the debate. The Soviet Union stressed the need to include economic and social rights in the bill. The American State Department was lukewarm toward that proposal. Mrs. Roosevelt's view was that while you could not set the individual apart from society, you should recognize that in any society the individual must have rights that are guarded. She saw no reason why economic and social rights should not be included in the draft bill, and managed to carry the State Department along with her.

Another difficult question was how binding the bill of

human rights should be. The smaller nations especially were not content with moral preaching. They wanted rights considered as a treaty obligation to be granted, protected, and enforced. Neither the United States nor the U.S.S.R. favored that. The solution was to create two documents, one a brief declaration of principles to provide a common standard of achievement, the other a precise covenant that would constitute a treaty binding on the states that ratified it, becoming a part of their own law.

On December 10, 1948, the draft declaration was finally adopted by the UN. Some cynics said it was absurd for an organization of governments to dedicate itself to protect human rights when everybody knew that all through history it was governments themselves which were the principal violators of those rights. But at least "the first step has been taken," said Mrs. Roosevelt. And as the years passed, the declaration would prove to have an influence far beyond expectations.

As for a covenant, action took much longer. Not until 1966 were two covenants, one on civil and political rights and the other on economic and social rights, approved by the UN General Assembly and opened for ratification. It took another decade to obtain the required number of ratifications. Both covenants became effective in 1976. (See Appendix for texts of the Universal Declaration of Human Rights and the two covenants.)

Beginning in 1948, then, with the adoption of the Universal Declaration, the legal foundation was firmly in place for an international standard of human rights.

A third of a century has passed since that day.

What is the condition of human rights now?

3

Junta Rule

Looking at the record, one disillusioned observer has remarked that "the only thing universal about human rights is their universal violation."

The facts bear this out: in 116 countries serious violations of human rights were reported during the year 1977. The figures come from the research arm of Amnesty International (AI). This worldwide organization is an independent group concerned exclusively with human rights. It works for the release of people jailed for their beliefs, provided they have not used or advocated violence. AI's survey was far from complete, for its work in the field of human rights related only to prisoners. Nor did it have the resources to do the thorough investigation needed in all countries.

The number of countries where violations occurred was alarming, said AI. And the situation was getting worse. "All major regions, all political or ideological blocs are involved, in spite of the Universal Declaration of Human Rights." Torture, declared unacceptable by the declaration, not only persists, but is even supported by governments. The declaration affirms the right to life; yet more than a hundred countries retain the death penalty. Even the governments which have ratified the legally binding international covenants on human rights—in force since 1976—are breaching them.

Not only governments, but political groups outside government—bands of terrorists, right-wing and left-wing—violate human rights daily. Individuals are taken as prisoners or hostages, and tortured and executed in the name of a political cause. Such violence done to human dignity and life is no more acceptable than repression by governments.

We have already had a glimpse of the situation in one country, Iran. (More will be said about Iran later, especially in connection with American foreign policy.) What about other places and other regimes? South of us is Latin America. As this book was being written, there were only three democracies surviving on the continent. Five other countries, Argentina, Chile, Bolivia, Paraguay, and Uruguay, make up a solid block of brutally repressive power. Violation of human rights in all of them is appallingly commonplace. One could choose any of them as an example of repression. Take Argentina. Hers is an ugly image, but unfortunately no worse than that of any military dictatorships on the southern cone of the continent.

On March 24, 1976, the military seized power in Argentina. The chiefs of the three armed services took supreme authority, appointing Lieutenant General Jorge Rafael Videla as President. Military men filled almost all the cabinet posts and administered all provincial and many local governments. Congress was disbanded and all political party activity suspended.

A small council of senior military officers advised the junta on lawmaking. One of its new laws provided the death penalty for crimes such as "disturbing the peace." The entire judiciary was replaced with military tribunals. Twenty-six million Argentineans were placed under martial law.

The coup came as no surprise. For twenty years Argentina had been the scene of a continuous struggle between weak civilian governments and a powerful military. There were constant outbreaks of terrorism, spiraling inflation threatened the economy, political imprisonment and kidnapping multiplied. Some observers thought the military might begin to solve the country's formidable problems. But what happened? Two years later the Center for International Policy (Washington, D.C.), a research group which analyzes U.S. foreign policy on human rights, reported that after taking power, the Argentine military government repeatedly claimed nearly all guerrilla activity had been liquidated. The two guerrilla groups, however, continued to carry out bombings, assassinations, kidnappings, and even full-scale battles. Victims of the military retribution killings were from groups considered suspect: labor leaders, intellectuals, foreigners, clergy, and friends or relatives of suspected guerrillas.

It has proved difficult to obtain identification of the people killed by the government's security forces. Bodies, often mutilated, are found on the beaches, floating in the rivers, at the bottom of lakes, decomposing in dumps, blown to pieces in quarries. On a visit to Buenos Aires late in 1977, Secretary of State Cyrus Vance delivered to Videla a list (compiled by a coalition of human rights groups) of 7,500 names of prisoners and missing people, said to represent at best only half the total number of victims of repression since the coup.

Three-quarters of the political prisoners have been neither charged nor tried. They are detained indefinitely under the control of the Executive Power. Although they are not supposed to be punished, according to the Argentinean constitution, they are held in punitive conditions. AI reports that many have been maltreated during transfers and the majority tortured as a matter of routine. (Such information is obtained from the statements of former prisoners and from documents written by detainees and smuggled out of prison.) Often prisoners are summarily executed, the authorities reporting that "they were shot while trying to escape." In one prison alone, at Cordoba, seventeen such executions took place in a three-month period.

Disappearances in Argentina are minimized by the government. It claims the so-called missing fall into three categories: those who choose to go "underground," those who emigrate, and those killed in clashes with security forces. But in many cases the abduction is witnessed by friends or relatives, which makes the official explanation doubtful, to say the least.

Precise figures are hard to get. Families fear reprisals, either against themselves or against the abducted person, if they should talk. Lawyers are pressured not to file writs of habeas corpus (the right to test the legality of confinement). Nevertheless, courageous lawyers do act, and courageous people do publicize the truth. To take but one example, the account of Rosa Daneman de Edelberg illustrates how such kidnappings usually occur:

Because of my advanced age, 72 years, I usually have with me my grandchildren, who each take it in turns to sleep with me for a week or two. At 1.00 o'clock in the morning of 15 July

[1976], plainclothed persons came to my house, bringing my son-in-law, Hugo Tarnopolsky, who knocked on the door and asked us to open it saying, "Open up, Nona, it's Hugo." When I opened it, I met my son-in-law and the plainclothes men who said they were the police and, with threats and blows, they asked for my grand-daughter, Bettina Tarnopolsky, who, for the reasons given before, had been sharing my house for a few days. After they had violently locked me out on the patio, I heard them taking away my grand-daughter, half-dressed, since most of her clothes were in her room. I also found, when I tried to contact my daughter Blanca Edelberg de Tarnopolsky, that these people who claimed to be policemen had ripped out the telephone, leaving me *incommunicado*. It took me some hours to recover from the physical and psychological violence of my unexpected visitors; then I went down to the street and rang my relatives from a public telephone, as it was impossible to contact my daughter. Together with one of my sons, I went to the home of my grand-daughter Bettina's parents, at Pena 2600, Dept A, Capital Federal, and found the front door completely destroyed and the place empty.

We asked the neighbours and the caretaker for information and found out that, some hours before the events at my house recounted above, plainclothes men, claiming to be police, asked the caretaker for the Tarnopolsky family and he showed them the apartment they lived in. When these policemen received no immediate response to their shouts from my grand-daughter's parents, the apartment door was blown open, so that they could enter straight away, to detain and take away my daughter and son-in-law. It was to be remembered that this took place before the events at my home.

I would also point out that my grandson Sergio Tarnopolsky —who was finishing compulsory military service at La Escuela de Mecanica de la Armada [Navy School of Mechanics]—has not returned home again, and is described as "disappeared" by the naval authorities. I have ascertained that on 14 July, Sergio rang his family saying that he was "confined to barracks."

I later discovered that Sergio's wife Laura had been abducted and/or detained by armed persons who raided her home.

Objective account of the facts so far: the disappearance of the whole Tarnopolsky family, Hugo and Blanca and their children Sergio and Bettina, and daughter-in-law Laura; the confiscation, robbery—or whatever it might be called—of valuables, including Hugo's car.

Charges of abduction, torture, disappearance, assassination, are sometimes not even denied by the authorities. They justify such actions on the grounds of a continuing state of war. The Minister of Foreign Affairs, Admiral César Guzzatti, said in 1976:

> My idea of subversion is that of the left-wing terrorist organizations. Subversion or terrorism of the right is not the same thing. When the social body of the country has been contaminated by a disease that corrodes its entrails, it forms antibodies. These antibodies cannot be considered in the same way as the microbes. As the government controls and destroys the guerrilla, the action of the antibody will disappear, as is already happening. It is only a natural reaction to a sick body.

Outrages have undoubtedly been committed by left-wing extremist groups. They have set off bombs in barracks and police stations, and have kidnapped and assassinated members of the military and business executives. But, says AI, "terrorist violence could not be held to justify the extreme and extensive government measures taken since the coup . . . There is overwhelming evidence that many innocent citizens have been tortured and have been killed. The actions taken against subversives have therefore been self-defeating: in order to restore security, an atmosphere of terror has been established; in order to counter illegal violence, legal safeguards have been removed and violent illegalities condoned."

Such a wave of repression is not limited to violence against the physical body. The war against ideas is just as deadly. The junta has systematically repressed intellectuals. Over two hundred scientists, artists, teachers, sociologists, writers, students are among the thousands of Argentines who have disappeared, been imprisoned without charge, or gone into exile. Refusal to espouse the "correct" political beliefs means blacklisting or worse. Actors are barred from stage, screen, television. Publishing houses are shut down, books are destroyed, newspapers are censored or suppressed. Sociology and psychology are considered dangerous fields to enter because they call for analysis of what is going on in society and in the mind. More than six hundred scientific staff in government research jobs were fired immediately after the coup. Research foundations relying on government funds were crippled by their withdrawal because the junta found them "filled with subversives."

All radio and television stations are directly controlled by the government. Grade schools are required to submit for approval lists of the books in their libraries. The fight against what the military conceives to be leftist subversion has brought almost total control of opinion. Those against the junta either say nothing or live in fear that something they say or do will bring personal disaster.

Perhaps the most eloquent witness to the violation of human

rights in Argentina is Rodolfo Walsh, one of his country's leading investigative journalists. He wrote an open letter to the junta which was published abroad. In it, he said in part:

Press censorship, the persecution of intellectuals, a recent police raid on my house, the murder of dear friends, and the loss of a daughter who died fighting the dictatorship, are some of the circumstances which oblige me to adopt this form of clandestine expression after having worked openly as a journalist during almost 30 years . . .

On 24 March 1976 you overthrew a government in which you had all participated, to whose disrepute you had contributed as the executors of its repressive policies, and whose limits were already defined by the elections due to be held six months later . . . What you liquidated was the possibility of a democratic process in which the people could have set right the evils which you had perpetuated and aggravated . . .

You have restored a totally bankrupt current of ideas representing the interests of an obsolete minority. This tiny minority blocks the development of our productive potential, exploits our people, and dismembers our country. Such a policy can be pursued, in the short term, by prohibiting political activity, taking over the trade unions, gagging the press, and spreading the most savage reign of terror Argentina has ever known.

Fifteen thousand people missing without trace, 10,000 prisoners, 4,000 dead, and tens of thousands of exiles are the statistical bones of this terror . . .

These events, which have already shaken the conscience of the civilized world, are not the greatest sufferings undergone by the Argentine people, nor the worst violations of human rights for which you are responsible. In the economic policies of the government, one finds not only the explanation of its repressive crimes, but also a greater atrocity which punishes millions of human beings with carefully planned misery . . .

These are the thoughts which I wished to share with the members of the junta on this first anniversary of your disreputable government, without hope of being listened to, in the certainty of persecution, but faithful to the commitment I made a long time ago to bear witness in difficult times.

The day after he wrote these words, Rodolfo Walsh was kidnapped from his home. He has not been seen since.

4

The New Order

On the far side of the world from Argentina is Indonesia, with another type of political regime—though just as repressive. It is the world's fifth most populous country, made up of a chain of thirteen thousand islands sprawling across the trade routes of the Pacific and Indian Oceans. A tide of repression and militarization has swept over Southeast Asia, engulfing Thailand, Malaysia, Singapore, the Philippines, and South Korea, as well as Indonesia. Although details may differ, what can be said of Indonesia's indifference to human rights could be said of all of them.

In Southeast Asia the vast majority of the people have traditionally been peasants. They lived a self-sustaining and simple life in the villages of the countryside. All these countries were under colonial rule for varying periods. Indonesian nationalists won independence from Dutch rule in 1949. For some time after independence the severe political repression known under the Dutch disappeared. But soon Indonesian politics began to polarize right and left. President Sukarno weakened parliamentary democracy by initiating martial law in 1957 and introducing a type of authoritarian rule he called "guided democracy." The great power it gave to the military was challenged by a rapidly growing Communist Party (PKI). The PKI soon numbered 3 million members and counted another 10 million Indonesians as its supporters in dozens of mass organizations. The PKI criticized the military's management of the economy and supported peasant efforts to expropriate land.

In 1965 a small group of left-wing army officers tried to overthrow the army leadership by assassinating several senior generals. The attempted coup was put down by the army, and a military regime under General Suharto took over from President Sukarno. The army carried out a massive and violent purge of people identified or suspected as Communists or subversives. Vast numbers were arrested, and of these, more than half a million were killed (a figure given out publicly in 1976 by Indonesia's chief of state security). A University of Indonesia study for the government reported as many as one million deaths.

To the toll of dead, add as the cost of repression another half million people thrown into prison and kept there. Dotting Indonesia today are scores of detention centers holding political prisoners without charge or trial. Observers estimate that between 55,000 and 100,000 have been confined ever since 1965.

A massive state security apparatus maintains watch over all aspects of Indonesian political and intellectual life. The effect is to prevent criticism of government policies. Constitutional and legal rights have been ignored. Sudden arrests, interrogation and torture, and the ever-present threat of summary execution or harsh and interminable imprisonment have made peaceful change or social progress almost impossible. Local military authorities rule their miniature despotisms. They have complete control over political prisoners. They can use them for forced labor, release and rearrest them at will. In the relatively few cases where political trials have occurred, normal judicial procedure is nonexistent and convictions have been reached on the flimsiest evidence, such as casual association with allegedly subversive elements. The courts have never yet acquitted a single defendant, and judges have handed out death sentences or gross terms of imprisonment. Such mock trials are designed to create an illusion of justice for the sake of international opinion.

The destructiveness of such arbitrary rule is hard to convey to the world outside. Perhaps this one small example will hint at the tragic consequences of this kind of regime. It is taken from a report by Amnesty International.

The prisoner, who cannot be named, was arrested early in 1966. Initially his wife was afraid to make inquiries about him for fear she too would be arrested. Later, she searched for him and failed to find him. The prisoner could not contact his family. The wife could not support her children and was forced to abandon their family home. She assumed her husband was dead.

One of their children was six years old when his father was taken away. He was especially devoted to his father. He became emotionally disturbed and obsessive about finding his father, and walked the streets asking strangers whether they had seen him. In early 1974, eight years after his father's arrest, he had grown into a boy of 14 who was mentally retarded, still obsessive and wandering from home in search of his father, showing passing strangers an old photograph. One day early in 1974, he walked by Salemba Prison in Jakarta and showed the photograph to a passing prison official. The boy thus found his father, after eight years. He was a prisoner in Salemba, where he had eventually been transferred.

What is life like for the prisoners themselves? The distinguished Indonesian lawyer Yap Thiem Hien, himself once a political prisoner, in defending a victim of government "justice," said to the court that political prisoners are "deprived of the most elementary rights enjoyed by all other citizens . . . They have no power and no voice, no right to complain or protest against their interminable imprisonment, against torture, insult, hunger or disease . . . Many of them have become automatons, going to sleep, getting up and taking their meals like persons without any spirit, for they are not permitted to read magazines, newspapers, or books, except religious literature. Nor are they allowed to write to their loved ones."

Some have become insane, he said, and others have committed suicide.

Indonesian prison conditions are grossly inadequate. Sanitation and washing facilities are very poor: in some cases prisoners who were issued one bar of soap in 1971 have never received another. Meager food—deficient in proteins and vitamins—taken together with extreme overcrowding and lack of medical care, have made tuberculosis endemic among prisoners. Malaria and intestinal diseases, too, have caused many deaths.

Late in 1976 the government announced a release program for the prisoners of 1965, to be spaced out over a three-year period. But that promise has turned into a nightmare for the prisoners and their families. After being held without trial for eleven years, people were transported to penal settlements remote from their homes. For this mock "release," an official cosmetic phrase was invented: "transmigration solution." The excuse given was that these prisoners must not be allowed to return to society jobless; that would create all kinds of danger, especially to "national security" and to "law and order." So by the thousands political prisoners were sent out to thinly populated and distant islands, there to undergo forced labor under harsh physical conditions.

On one such island, Buru, at least fourteen thousand prisoners are now held in some eighteen camps. Buru is in an easterly group of Indonesia's islands. It is mountainous and covered with dense jungle. Agriculture is in a primitive stage. No roads link the small capital town with the tiny villages. There is almost no regular communication with the rest of Indonesia. The prisoners were transferred in secrecy and haste, with no time to say goodbye to their families. At their new sites there was no housing or transportation. They were forced to build the camps and make the rafts and carts needed for traveling along the river and jungle tracks. There was no food until they cleared fields in the jungle and planted them with rice, maize, cassava, and vegetables. The supplies are so limited that they eat snakes, mice, rats, and dogs to survive. It is no mystery that the death rate on the penal island is high.

Indonesia ratified the International Convention on forced labor in 1950. The signators agreed not to permit within their borders any system of forced labor. Early in the twentieth century the use of forced labor, which is merely slavery under another name, had become an organic part of totalitarian regimes. Widespread arrests placed the labor of citizens at the disposal of the state. Although Indonesia signed the agreement, it was nevertheless reported in 1976 that Indonesia's political prisoners were "performing forced or compulsory labor within the meaning of the Convention."

There is little contact allowed between prisoners and their families. Mail rarely reaches the camps, and when it does, it may be half a year late. Few parcels from the family arrive, and although visits are not officially prohibited, none have ever taken place. The authorities encourage prisoners' families to live on Buru, but the small number who have chosen to do so find they must live and work under the same brutal conditions as the prisoners.

Only the hardiest and most optimistic soul entrapped by Indonesia's interpretation of "national security" can retain hope of knowing justice someday. To bring the prisoners to trial and release those against whom no charge could be made would have been a step toward recognition of human rights. Instead, President Suharto's "New Order" turned to long-term compulsory resettlement. "Resettlement" community? The correct term is concentration camp.

Women as well as men suffer imprisonment without trial under the Suharto regime. AI estimates probably two thousand women are being held in women's prisons throughout the archipelago. Many are girls who were in their early teens when arrested in 1965. A number of them are illiterate. A typical example is Walmijati, a medical auxiliary who worked in a Jakarta hospital. She was about fifteen in 1965. Probably her arrest came because she belonged to a leftist youth movement. Severely beaten during interrogation, her injuries brought about mental illness. Nevertheless, she was sent to a women's prison where she has been ever since, without trial. Her family is poor and cannot afford to visit her in prison.

The wives and children of political prisoners suffer even beyond the expected pain of forced separation from their loved ones. They, too, are treated as though guilty—guilty by association. The atmosphere of suspicion is so intense that people fear contact with anyone linked to those condemned by the authorities. For many years "Certificates of Non-involvement" in the attempted coup of 1965 were a prerequisite for entry to school, for getting a job, or for moving from one district to another. Although they are no longer officially required, the local military still demands the equivalent. Even foreign firms sometimes ask for such certificates when interviewing job applicants.

Few prisoners' wives can have regular jobs under such conditions. They try to survive as domestic servants, by selling homemade products in market stalls, or by making dresses. If they know where their husbands are imprisoned, they bring them food they can hardly spare. The cost of simply staying alive, of keeping the family going, is an enormous burden.

Even in those relatively few cases where a political prisoner is released, his fate is still grim. He must spend a year or more under "town arrest," reporting regularly to the military. He has to have a known and fixed address as a precondition for release, an insuperable obstacle for many prisoners whose families have disappeared or been destroyed during his long absence. The ex-prisoner, labeled a permanent suspect, is denied work, which places an additional burden on his family. Friends and neighbors shun association with him for fear of attracting the attention of the security police. The government feeds the controlled press, radio, and television false reports and instills such fear that there is widespread ignorance of the true conditions of political prisoners. Better not to know, or even to think about the problem, when the consequences of "meddling" are so dangerous.

Nevertheless, some are courageous enough to "meddle." Yap Thiem Hien, the lawyer, imprisoned for eleven months without charge or trial and then freed, was cautioned by the chief of internal security to stick to his profession and not meddle in politics. But Mr. Yap, a member of the International Commission of Jurists and a hero to opponents of the Suharto regime, has never agreed to be silent. He speaks his mind openly to journalists. In one interview he said there can be no human rights without the rule of law. He cited such deficiencies in Indonesian legislation as an absence of habeas corpus or the right to bail, the unlimited right of courts to hold prisoners without charge or trial, and the lack of right to counsel except in capital cases (those for which the punishment is death). Most common-law defendants are tried without counsel. (There are only five hundred practicing lawyers for a population of about 135 million.)

But how would it be possible to institute rule of law when the parliament is tightly controlled by Suharto? It would require raising the political consciousness of the people. Yet half the people are illiterate or semiliterate, "for ages subject to all kinds of extortion and oppression from their own chiefs in feudal times and now from the new feudalism." Candidates for parliament are screened, criticism of government policy is prohibited, and voters are intimidated. The government won't permit the freedom to raise the understanding of law and human rights. "We're in a vicious circle," Mr. Yap said. "That's why some student groups say talking doesn't help any more.

They tell me, 'We respect your idea of non-violence, but we see as a last resort only action, any kind of action.'

"We have a situation where the Government is not inclined to tolerate dissent, at least not publicly voiced. All human rights derive from this. Freedom is stated in the Constitution, but in the implementation they demand 'responsible freedom,' and of course they reserve the right to say whether it's 'responsible' or not."

The problem of poverty, Mr. Yap believes, is at the bottom of the question of human rights in his country. Attached to it is the problem of illiteracy and ignorance of law. The poor "will always be the victims of people who have better educational, social and economic positions and who hold the power of law enforcement."

Here is an example of the intimate connection between the two classes of human rights—the civil and political, and the social and economic. Indonesians have enjoyed little of either. In the boom-town capital of Jakarta and other cities, modern high-rise buildings tower over sprawling slum districts. Mercedes-Benz cars purr through the streets, and "the initials of Pierre Cardin are worn like a badge of new riches by sleek men and women in public places." But 60 percent of the population is malnourished, reports the Health Ministry. The average yearly meat consumption per person is 8.4 pounds, compared with 176 pounds in the United States. The average Indonesian drinks a pint of milk a year (roughly what an American drinks in one day) and eats only eleven eggs a year. Infant mortality on the island of Java, where 80 million live, is between 130 and 144 per 1,000. That is thirty to forty times higher than in the West. A fifth of the children born in Java do not reach five years of age.

Most Indonesians live at or below the poverty line, and the gap between rich and poor is increasing. The authoritarian Suharto government has emphasized economic development, based on the extraction of Indonesia's vast natural resources— oil, minerals, timber, rubber, coffee. But the value of that development has not reached the majority. As in most of Southeast Asia, the military government cooperates with the domestic and multinational corporations (dominated by those based in the United States and Japan) and the profiteering does not improve the well-being of the people.

Influenced by modern advertising methods, farm families of Indonesia have given up the traditional soybean meal to eat the status food—white bread—which is much less nutritious. Baby-food corporations, expanding their markets, have hired nurses and nurse's aides to persuade mothers to abandon breast feeding in favor of the "more modern and convenient" use of baby formulas and foods. Junk foods—"Coke colonization"—spread like the plague.

In such developing nations the people are commonly told that bread is more important than liberty. But in a country under one-man rule or a military clique, who will decide how the bread will be distributed? Can you have a fair share of bread if you are not free?

To maximize the profits of a developing economy, owners and managers try to keep labor costs as low as possible on the land, in the mines, and in the factories. The rights of workers and farmers are severely limited under authoritarian regimes eager to cooperate with the corporations. In most such countries unions have been coopted or emasculated, strikes and boycotts forbidden, and militant leaders jailed or killed.

What the experts and technocrats think about the problem

is revealed in a study done by a business advisory group, the International Development Center of Japan, in 1973: "Indonesia has a bright future in her path of industrialization due to her rich resources such as cheap labor." That view of labor as just another resource to be exploited indicates little sympathy for or understanding of human rights. It can only contribute to the dehumanization of Indonesians.

The younger students and intellectuals of Indonesia, and recently even some officials, have grown suspicious of the international technocrats involved in development projects. Like the older Indonesians who experienced colonialism, they see that "what has been built serves mainly the needs of the foreign investors and the Government, not the people of Indonesia . . . They are not really interested in the well-being of the people. They are indifferent to human rights and the rule of law. They will work for anybody who puts them there."

Corruption accounts in part for economic injustice. It is widespread in Southeast Asia, where tradition requires that people moving into positions of privilege consider their first responsibility to be to family and friends, not to the enterprise, the government, or the general welfare. This tradition made it all the easier for corporations accustomed to corruption as a tool of business. In Jakarta, businessmen figure about 30 percent as "unreceiptable expenses." And the same percentage has been estimated as the portion of the state budget which goes into private pockets. The fact that in two years the state-owned oil company, Pertamina, went bankrupt bears eloquent witness to the extent of official corruption. Rumors about who is taking what from whom flood business and government circles. The elite and the bureaucracy fatten on corruption at the expense of the people.

Criticism of the Indonesian and other regimes in Southeast Asia has been nearly silenced. Only in guarded private conversations or in secret and illegal meetings are the facts voiced. Journalists are intimidated, fired, exiled, jailed, killed. Publishers or broadcasters who depend upon advertising or the government's good will cannot antagonize the powerful.

Who can tell the people the truth about how they are being robbed of their social and economic rights? No one, in a state system which also denies the people their political and civil rights.

5

Rule by Race

There is only one country in the world which *by law* denies human, political, and economic rights to its citizens, purely on the basis of race.

That country is South Africa.

The system of discriminatory racial legislation the ruling white minority has imposed upon the people is called *apartheid*.

Its advocates claim that it provides for the separate but parallel development of peoples whose skins are of a different color. But in 1973, twenty-five years after apartheid had been introduced, the UN General Assembly declared it "a crime against humanity."

A quick look at the history of South Africa will help make clear what apartheid means and how it came about. The first permanent white settlement in what is now South Africa was established by the Dutch East India Company in the 1650s. At that time the people commonly known as Bushmen lived in the

Cape area and the more numerous Bantu-speaking peoples farther north. The white settlers—British as well as Dutch—expanded their areas slowly at first, but by the late nineteenth century they dominated almost all of what is now South Africa. They created a racially stratified society, the whites in command and the indigenous African population treated much like serfs.

With the discovery of diamond and gold deposits at the turn of the century, the traditional agricultural economy began to shift to mining and industry. The competitive British colonies and the Afrikaner republics clashed in the Boer War of 1899, with the British winning complete rule. The Union of South Africa was soon set up as a virtually independent commonwealth under the Crown. In 1961, the link with Great Britain was broken; South Africa became a republic and left the Commonwealth.

The diamond and gold mines drew great numbers of African migrant workers. As they became the indispensable labor force, their tribal ties weakened and their political rights were whittled away to ensure white control.

When the Afrikaner Nationalists (the descendants of the original Dutch settlers) came to power in 1948, they cemented many of the already-existing discriminatory practices into an apartheid program. The writer Dan Jacobson, born and raised in South Africa, recalls that the Afrikaners took over with two intentions. "One was to insure the dominance of their language and culture vis-à-vis the English-speaking whites; the other was to see to it that the white man in general, and the Afrikaners in particular, would continue to keep in subjection the country's blacks, Colored (mulattoes), and Indians . . ."

The Afrikaner governments wiped out whatever rights of

representation the "non-whites" then had. They turned old practices of racial discrimination "into a pattern of punitive legislation which governed everything from post-office entrances to areas of habitation for the different races, or from the kind of job you were permitted to take to the kind of person you were permitted to marry." It was very much like Nazi Germany's racism.

The laws which constitute apartheid are not edicts issued by any dictator. They are the product of party discussion (white) and of parliamentary decision (white). Pieced together over the years, the system has divided the country so that 4 million whites, only one-sixth of the population, have control over 87 percent of the country—including all the major urban, industrial, and mining centers, as well as most of the good farmland. Blacks are allocated only 13 percent of the land—divided into ethnic "homelands." Half of the 18 million blacks live in Soweto and similar townships on the fringes of industrial centers, where they are denied all political rights. The blacks who live in such "white" areas, where they are the mainstay of the economy, are regarded as "temporary" residents, even when they have been born there. They are not permitted to own land or to move about freely; they must carry identity documents—passbooks—at all times.

What effect does apartheid have on the living conditions of the Africans? The state of physical and mental health is always an index to the socio-economic standards of a country. Malnutrition, virtually unknown among white children of South Africa, is endemic among blacks. A late 1970s survey of Mdanstane, a black township outside the coastal city of East London, showed that 68 percent of the black children under five were suffering from malnutrition. Another study, made by the University of Pretoria, estimated that every day seventy-five nonwhite children in South Africa die from malnutrition. Or take tuberculosis. In 1974, 1.8 whites in 10,000 suffered from TB, against 27.9 blacks and 32.5 of those of mixed race.

Overcrowding and poverty among blacks accounts in large part for the heavy incidence of diabetes, rheumatic heart disease, hypertension, scabies, diarrhea, infectious kidney disease, and the eye afflictions trachoma and glaucoma. These in addition to malnutrition and TB. Medical studies also point to chronic alcoholism and the high rate of traumatic injuries among blacks as products of the social environment—or, to put it another way, as products of the deprivation of social and economic rights.

Although there is an exceptionally good medical facility for blacks in Soweto—the Baragwanath General Hospital—South Africa's medical system at large favors whites over nonwhites. The government spends disproportionately high sums on medical facilities for whites only, and pays higher salaries to white professional staff than to nonwhite. It provides one hospital bed for every 98 whites, as against one for every 179 nonwhites, although the disease and accident rates are far higher among nonwhites.

By chopping the country into ethnic territories which are supposed to become autonomous and fully independent nation-states, protecting the identity of each ethnic group, the nationalists say they have devised the ideal system for South Africa. But "separate development," the whole world has observed, is a sham. It is a transparent method of "divide and rule," totally without moral justification. The black South Africans were never asked what they wanted: ethnic territories were ordained by the whites, without any choice permitted the blacks by vote or referendum. Apartheid was an obvious way to maintain white political supremacy and to preserve white social and economic privilege. The policy of the South African government was designed to perpetuate a system in which the white minority gets a grossly disproportionate share of the country's wealth. And that wealth is considerable: South Africa is the most richly endowed country on the continent.

From the beginning of white settlement, African tribal groups resisted territorial encroachment and white domination. But they resisted as separate tribal groups rather than as a people united by a common cultural and linguistic heritage. Not until the early 1900s did African resistance to white rule organize across tribal lines or with a national consciousness. Out of the small black middle class came the African National Congress (ANC), which tried to improve the position of the Western-educated Africans, rather than to speak for the needs of the majority blacks. It was after World War II, and especially after the nationalists took power in 1948 and began to codify apartheid, that the ANC developed a political program with mass support. Campaigns of passive resistance and defiance of discriminatory legislation brought mass arrests and repression. Joining with the Asian and colored peoples and with white progressives, the blacks drew up a Freedom Charter, pressing for change by nonviolent methods. Again the government responded with arrests and trials of the leaders of the protesting organizations.

By the end of the 1950s, there was growing disillusionment with what nonviolent resistance could accomplish. At Sharpeville in 1960, police opened fire without provocation on unarmed Africans demonstrating against the restrictive pass laws. Scores of Africans were killed. Protest demonstrations throughout South Africa were met with emergency decrees and the banning of the ANC and the newer Pan-African Congress (PAC). Robert Sobukwe, the PAC leader, was arrested and jailed. Convinced now that change could be achieved only by violent means, many black political leaders helped form a military wing of the underground nationalist movement. In 1963 Nelson Mandela and other nationalist leaders were imprisoned, and an armed struggle began with the goal of overthrowing white minority rule.

In the early 1970s, the young, the educated, and the urban Africans began to develop a Black Consciousness movement. It stressed the need for black solidarity to achieve a stronger bargaining position with the white minority. The leaders helped create community programs for self-education and self-help. Their organizations were not suppressed immediately by the government. Instead, many of the leaders were subjected to banning, detention, and imprisonment. Rapidly the movement won wide support and became a major force in South African politics. Since June 1976, when high-school students began peaceful demonstrations in Soweto, protesting use of Afrikaans as the official teaching language, more than eight hundred people have been shot in the streets, thousands have been arrested, and a number have died in detention. In October 1977, the government banned all the Black Consciousness organizations.

How does the system of apartheid function? Africans have no citizenship rights in the republic; those rights can be exercised only within their assigned homeland areas (*bantustans*). The tribal groupings have limited powers of self-government in the bantustans. The requirements for citizenship in these territories were set by the South African government in the first place, not by the people themselves.

By holding tight to the reins of power, the white minority is able to distribute the country's resources between the white and black communities in a grossly unequal way. It has adopted laws to prevent African advancement in those spheres —labor and education—which could equalize benefits. Blacks are prevented from entering certain categories of skilled work, and from receiving higher education in the universities. Yet, after designing a social structure to keep blacks politically and economically backward, the government offers as an excuse for withholding equal rights the fact that the blacks are politically backward. A more absurd and vicious argument would be hard to find.

As a result of apartheid, the South African economy is held back by the mere subsistence allowed the blacks. The low wages paid black labor reduce the potential consumers' market; and the 2 million black unemployed (a number expanding yearly by 200,000 young people) are another grave sign of economic and political trouble.

Perhaps the most glaring example of the effect of apartheid is the plight of the African migrant worker. There are about 1.5 million of them; they help staff the mines, factories, and businesses that have made South Africa wealthy. (The government argument that it was the whites who built South Africa into a modern industrial state is a lie, for nothing was ever made or built in the country without black labor, black labor paid at the lowest rate.)

More than the other blacks, the migrants are prisoners of the "pass laws." That web of restrictions confines most blacks to the tribal homeland. Nearly 10 million of the 18 million blacks make their permanent home on these reservations. In the past, they survived on subsistence farming, but the traditional livelihood has been undermined by chronic overcrowding of what arable land there is. Population density in some of the smaller homelands now matches that of the poorest parts of Asia.

With their families desperately poor, men of working age usually seek permission from the labor bureau to migrate to the white areas, where most of the cash-paying jobs are. But only a small percentage make it, and if they do, it means leaving their families behind for months or even years. Their restricted life on the fringes of the white industrial areas is grim: dingy, overcrowded barracks; beds without mattresses; gambling, drink, and prostitutes as the only relief from labor; and almost no chance to climb up the economic ladder. "We live just like monkeys in a cage," one migrant worker put it.

Such "temporary" residents may be sent back to their tribal homeland at any time. Under the laws they must carry passes specifying where they live and work. To travel outside these areas without permission or to fail to produce a pass on demand is a punishable offense. More than 250,000 have been prosecuted and many are imprisoned each year.

Apartheid's violation of fundamental human rights was bound to cause black resistance. The government has wide powers to control and suppress all forms of political opposition. Parties and organizations can be banned, public meetings prohibited, newspapers and other forms of expression silenced. How people are harassed and detained for their conscientious opposition to the repressive government reflects the nature of the South African legal and punitive system. The state has devised many means to serve its repressive ends.

First, there are the security laws, which apply both to those convicted and those as yet untried. One of these laws, the Terrorism Act, casts an enormous net over all attempts to achieve social or political change, or any activity which may be said to endanger law and order. Dangers to the maintenance of law and order are defined in ridiculously broad terms. You risk being accused of terrorism if you do something which results in "disturbance or disorder," in "prejudice" to "any industry or undertaking," in causing "financial loss to any person or the State," in increasing "hostility between the White and other inhabitants of the Republic," in obstructing the "free movement of any traffic on land, at sea or in the air," or in embarrassing "the administration of the affairs of the State."

The accused in such cases has to prove his innocence, rather than the state having to demonstrate his guilt. Minimum sentence is five years; maximum: death. The police can arrest suspects without warrant or charge and hold them incommunicado indefinitely.

The Internal Security Act provides for preventive detention, the imposition of banning orders, and the detaining of potential state witnesses in political trials. The Minister of Justice can ban anyone who endangers the state's security and hold them for twelve months without trial. Such detention is used to intimidate opponents of apartheid. The system of detention permits seizing helpless people who are not allowed access to lawyers, family, or friends—access not even denied a criminal. The practice is not reserved for times of crisis. It is an everyday means of smothering political opposition and strengthening minority rule.

Although the constitution calls for separation of powers, several of the security laws cannot be challenged in court, especially detention ordered under the Treason Act or banning orders issued under the Internal Security Act. Despite the limits placed on their freedom of decision, South African judges have not tried to secure repeal of unjust laws; they almost invariably uphold them.

The banning power allows the minister to place under house arrest, with restricted freedom of movement, association, and expression, anyone suspected of actions taken against the maintenance of public order. The targets include trade-union organizers and the political leaders of the black community. These orders may be reimposed many times. It often happens that a prisoner who has served a full term of ten years may then immediately have a banning order placed upon him, generally for five years. This usually means the victim cannot practice his or her profession; thus families are sentenced to extreme hardship.

Banishment is used by the government to separate political leaders from their followers and to make communication between leaders more difficult. The oppositionists are forced to move to the most remote corners of the vast country, at times without their families, and often where the native language is not their own and where work is hard to find. The separation brings poverty as well as isolation from family and friends.

What the government did to Stephen Biko indicates how murderously resistant the white Afrikaner rulers are to any proposals for change in apartheid. Biko had stepped into the leadership vacuum left when Nelson Mandela,* head of the ANC, and Robert Sobukwe,* head of the PAC, were jailed. A founder of the Black Consciousness movement, young Biko was banned for five years in 1973. In August 1977 he was

---

* *Mandela is serving a sentence of life imprisonment; Sobukwe died in detention.*

arrested at a security-police roadblock while breaking the banning order. Scores of political prisoners who had been taken in for police interrogation had died during the proceedings. But when Biko was picked up for this, the fourth time, there was not the same fear that he would be treated violently. His prominence, his friends thought, would give him immunity from police violence. Not an extremist, Biko called for dismantling the apartheid system to facilitate the organization of a black vanguard that would lead the fight for a nonracial society and eventual black majority rule. He advocated nonviolent solutions, but if the government failed to let down the apartheid bars, he was ready to force it to the bargaining table through violent disruption of the national economy.

A few weeks after his arrest, Biko was chained to a grille and subjected to twenty-two hours of interrogation, during which he suffered blows to his head that caused brain damage. He died six days later in a coma, naked on the floor of a cell. He was thirty years old.

Only international anger at the horrifying fate of Stephen Biko forced the government to make an inquiry—however hypocritical—into his death in detention. At the conclusion of the official inquiry, the security police interrogators were cleared of any responsibility for his death.

Stephen Biko's case is but one example of harsh treatment in prison, often ending in death. Torture is a routine practice of the security police; the government denies either that it occurs or that it has official sanction. But reports by AI and other organizations on torture contain many statements from former prisoners about brutal treatment, accompanied by photographs or autopsy reports.

In testimony given January 1978 before the U.S. Congressional Ad Hoc Monitoring Group on South Africa, AI concluded by saying:

> Apartheid is part of the definition of life in South Africa. For the African particularly, there are few areas of life which are untouched by the severe restriction of human rights. Freedom of expression, freedom of movement, freedom of choice remain largely mythical ideas in a society in which association is treated with suspicion, ambition with distrust, equality with venom. Apartheid is an intricate, though not subtle, justification for continuing the domination of the black majority in South Africa by its white minority. Its existence is a denial of human rights and fundamental freedoms; until it goes, South Africa remains a society in chains.

6

An Empire of Cogs

Argentina . . . Indonesia . . . South Africa . . . These are the countries described so far in this book. Each an authoritarian regime, each violating human rights on an immense scale. And each placed on the right of the political spectrum.

But what about countries on the left—the Communist regimes? They can be defined as those in which all power is in the hands of a single party which calls itself Communist. Is their record on human rights any different from the right-wing regimes?

By far the oldest of such regimes is the Union of Soviet Socialist Republics. The U.S.S.R. has been in existence for over sixty years. Born in the Revolution of 1917, it was briefly a coalition democracy with several political parties functioning. Within months, when the elections went against the Communists, they took power in a coup and made all other parties illegal.

In all authoritarian regimes opposition is suppressed, though they may differ in the degree to which the state controls all aspects of the society. Both right and left authoritarian regimes stand in contrast to democratic societies—those committed to the principle of government by the freely expressed consent of the governed, and to the conditions of free discussion necessary to the expression of that consent. Democracies too, of course, vary in the degree to which they fulfill that commitment in practice. But their essence, political freedom, remains. And that simply means guaranteeing each citizen an institutionalized means of exerting a fair share of influence upon the selection of his government and the policies it is to follow.

The one-party states commonly assert a greater concern for social and economic progress than for civil and political rights. They say such rights are a luxury they cannot afford until their societies achieve the standard of living necessary to sustain political liberty. Take Iran. Responding to criticism of tyranny in his country, Jahangir Amuzegar, Iran's representative to the International Monetary Fund and the World Bank, said that respect was owed those nations "where certain political niceties are sacrificed, and certain libertarian corners are cut, in order to assure maximum economic growth." In other words, let's feed people first, and then worry about freedom of expression.

But is that simply an excuse for repression? An excuse for the freedom to exploit others? In a society in which there is no freedom of thought and expression, can there be social justice? Are not debate and diversity essential to truth and progress? Do not tyrannies of the right or left come inevitably to be managed by the few for their own ends?

In coming to grips with these questions, it may help to look at the condition of human rights in Soviet Russia. One must recognize that differences in history, in tradition, in ideological values shape a country's political life. Certainly no tradition of freedom can be found in Russia's past. Since the thirteenth century Russia has pursued a path different from Europe's. From Alexander Nevsky's day it has known only a harshly centralized style of rule. It never went through a feudal stage of development. In contrast to the rest of Europe, no self-assertive aristocracy arose to challenge the absolute rights of the sovereign over the land and its people. Ivan the Terrible eliminated the restless barons who in England forced a Magna Carta upon King John. In Russia there is no tradition of any social class rising to political ascendancy. Even when Peter the Great brutally "Europeanized" Russia in the eighteenth century, his aim was to import the material achievements of Western Europe, not to introduce the critical spirit of free inquiry that gave birth to them. The state continued its absolute rule over the country. Nor with the Bolshevik Revolution was genuine democracy achieved. Power was still as absolute, only now it was in the hands of a new authority, the all-embracing bureaucratic state.

Throughout most of Russia's history, opposition to the state has been considered a crime. The punishment has generally been prison, exile, confinement in a labor camp, or death. After the Revolution of 1917, the police-state methods of the czar were continued by the Communist leaders and made even more efficient in stamping out unorthodox ways. Those suspected of opposition or dissidence were removed from their office or their jobs by the secret police. People were arrested, and sentenced without trial. Such administrative justice became normal in the Soviet Union.

As the new leaders struggled to consolidate their positions after 1917, arrests occurred on a larger and larger scale. Many people were taken into custody as a preventive measure. That is, a person was arrested not because he had done something but because there was something about his personality, his social origins, his family, friends, or associates, even about his home, that suggested he *might* do something harmful to the state. Any sign interpreted as potential disloyalty could lead to what has been called "prophylactic" arrest.

The opportunities for getting rid of personal enemies, for settling grudges, for putting away rivals in love or on the job, for taking over a better apartment, are all too easy. In such a climate citizens become supersensitive to every mood, word, act, or relationship that might place them in danger. Terror blankets everyday life. The fear of running afoul of the law strangles initiative, imagination, and enterprise. The threat of the secret police is constantly on people's minds. The reality of forced labor camps and the risk of being committed to one of them are powerful means of controlling the population and suppressing dissent.

The forced labor of convicts, common in Czarist Russia, increased enormously under the Soviets. Slave labor became a significant factor in Stalin's regime. He used millions of political prisoners on a great variety of projects, especially in Siberia, Central Asia, and above the Arctic Circle. In the gold-mining labor camps of Arctic Siberia, the worst part of the Soviet concentration-camp system, 3 million people are known to have died. Students of Soviet affairs have estimated that from several million to 25 million were victims of the system. A probable figure, many hold, is that in the U.S.S.R. at any one time some 5 to 8 million people were in "corrective labor camps." Alexander Solzhenitsyn—who himself spent eleven years of his life in prison, in concentration camps, and in exile in the Soviet Union—in his three-volume *Gulag Archipelago* has taken the faceless statistics of the terror and made the vast suffering and destruction recognizably human to us.

Within a year of Stalin's death in 1953, many political prisoners were released from the labor camps and the prisons. Khrushchev's denunciation of Stalin in his speech of 1956 to the Twentieth Party Congress and the implied promise of a more open society led Soviet intellectuals to hope for a continued liberalization. That was the period when for the first time one could talk and write about the labor camps and the terror. Solzhenitsyn's novel *One Day in the Life of Ivan Denisovich* was published, as well as many other literary works of a kind that had been totally censored in the past. In 1968, however, after Soviet-led troops crushed the movement for "Socialism with a human face" in Czechoslovakia, the hope of opening Soviet society was abandoned by many.

True, the death camps did not return. Summary executions are no longer commonplace. Mass repressions are avoided. There is an attempt to give the appearance of due legal process. But men and women are still being committed to prison, to labor camps, to internal exile, to psychiatric prisons, for insisting on their rights as defined in Soviet law, for defending human rights and their own dignity. The system, still monolithic, leaves no room for human freedom. The relentless demand for conformity cramps human faculties. Setting abstractions above individuals, the state has acted as though its citizens do not want or understand freedom.

But that there is an almost instinctive need to assert one's rights insofar as they have been officially defined is demonstrated regularly in the Soviet Union. For more than ten years now there has been a democratic movement, made up of dissidents. It is not a big movement, from all accounts, nor is it organized like a political party. Some dissidents would like to see their government respect its own constitution, which guarantees the citizen certain rights. Some would like to see far-reaching reforms in Soviet society, perhaps akin to the liberalizing tendencies expressed in the Czech "Spring" of 1968, that brief period when the government itself encouraged the turn toward "Socialism with a human face." Others would simply like the right to comment on the system freely.

What explains the presence of such a movement today? Max Hayward, an editor and translator of Soviet dissident writing, observes that with "penalties much less Draconian than the instant, inglorious extinction visited on would-be dissenters in Stalin's day, far greater numbers of people are drawn to give expression to their innate sense of truth." It was in the mid-1960s that dissent began on a scale which the authorities could not conceal. The 1965 trial of writers Andrei Sinyavsky and Yuli Daniel "had an effect on the Soviet educated public similar to that of the Dreyfus case in France at the end of the last century. There is no independent press in which a Russian Zola could have pronounced his *J'Accuse!* but letters of protest against the sentences, typed out in many copies and signed by an astonishingly large number of intellectuals willing to risk arrest or, at the very least, loss of livelihood, circulated from hand to hand in Moscow."

That was the birth of *samizdat*—"self-publication." It revealed to the outside world that free thought in Russia was not dead. It had somehow survived decades of repression.

Samizdat literature has become the alternative press in the Soviet Union. On one side are the official newspapers, magazines, and books, issued under the stamp of the censor. On the other side are the countless self-published writings which try to provide a picture of the Soviet Union as it really is. Because samizdat is the forum for free opinion and a display case for fact unprocessed by the official censor, it is a threat to the ruling elite. It encompasses all forms of expression. Through samizdat the citizen can read leaflets, newspapers, journals, novels, poetry, essays, manifestoes. The typewriter is the basic means of production, but in use, too, are the photography process and, more rarely, underground printing presses.

The main source of information on the dissident movement has been the *Chronicle of Current Events.* It began in 1968, inspired by the Prague "Spring," and was soon followed by many samizdat journals voicing the non-official views of nationalists, religious groups, political thinkers, human rights advocates. Samizdat publication is open to anyone with courage, an idea, and information. All one needs is a typewriter, friends to distribute the copy, and readers who welcome independent views. So long as Soviet citizens have opinions displeasing to the Party and the KGB, the vehicle of their thoughts will be samizdat, the only free press in the U.S.S.R.

The single most consistent and prominent Soviet voice for human rights has been that of the distinguished theoretical physicist Andrei Sakharov. In the late 1940s, when still in his twenties, he had an important role in the development of the hydrogen bomb, and he was made a member of the prestigious Academy of Sciences at the age of thirty-two. At first he felt the Soviet bomb would foster the balance of power and therefore contribute to peace. But then he said, "I gradually began to understand the criminal nature not only of nuclear tests but of the enterprise as a whole. I beagn to look on it and on other world problems from a broader, more humane perspective." In a 1968 essay published abroad—but circulated at home only in samizdat—he argued for a convergence of the capitalist West and the socialist East as the way to avoid mankind's destruction. That cost him his security clearance and shut him off from work in his own field. He became more involved with dissidents, signing petitions for the release of arrested intellectuals, standing vigil at political trials, keeping the Western press posted on the dissident movement. In 1970 he joined with physicist Valentin Turchin and historian Roy Medvedev in an appeal for gradual democratization and took the initiative in founding a Human Rights Committee in Moscow. When he was awarded the Nobel Peace Prize in 1975, the Kremlin denied him an exit visa to make the journey to accept the prize.

Despite great hardship, Sakharov has remained at the center of Soviet dissidence, offering counsel and giving sanctuary. Only his great international prestige has saved him, thus far, from prison, labor camp, or exile. But other dissenters have suffered swift retaliation for their courage. Their only shield has been responsiveness to their case by people in the West. At times the Soviet government's harshness toward dissidence seems inhibited by Western public opinion and by considerations of foreign policy. It may soften for a time its position on emigration or artistic freedom or political criticism. But when relations with the United States are not good, then American disapproval seems to carry little weight. And tough action is taken against dissidents.

The spring and summer of 1978 was such a time of persecution. Here, in brief form, as reported in the Western press, is what happened to Soviet dissidents:

· Miroslav Marinovich and Mikola Matusevich, members of a dissident group in Kiev monitoring Soviet compliance with the Helsinki accord on human rights (see Appendix), were sentenced to seven years in prison to be followed by five years of exile in Siberia. That brought to 22 the number of those in monitoring groups to be arrested in the past 14 months.

· Grigory Golshtein, a member of a monitoring group in Tbilisi, capital of Soviet Georgia, was sentenced to a year in prison for "parasitism," the Soviet term of joblessness. (He lost his job in 1971 when he applied to emigrate to Israel.)

· Vladimir Shelkov, the 82-year-old leader of the Seventh Day Adventists who can function only underground, was arrested in Tashkent.

· Yakov N. Dolgoter, a 19-year-old Adventist, was seized in Pyatigorsk and beaten repeatedly by agents of the KGB, the secret police, trying to get from him the names of other underground Adventists.

· Kirill Podrabinek, 25, brother of Aleksandr Podrabinek, 24, head of a dissident group publicizing abuses of psychiatry for political purposes, was given a sentence of two-and-a-half years on an allegedly false charge of possessing rifle ammunition.

· Aleksandr Podrabinek was arrested and charged with "anti-Soviet slander" for his book, *Punitive Psychiatry*. Earlier he had been ordered to emigrate, but since he did not wish to, refused.

· Mstislav Rostropovich, cellist, and his wife, the soprano Galina Vishnevskaya, who had been living in the West for four years, were stripped of their Soviet citizenship for "un-patriotic activity" and barred from returning home.

· General Pyotr G. Grigorenko, a World War II hero who turned into a political dissident, in New York for surgery, had his Soviet citizenship taken away for "damaging the prestige of the USSR."

· Vladimir Slepak, 50-year-old engineer, was sentenced to five years in exile in a remote area for "malicious hooliganism." As Jews, he and his wife had been trying to emigrate to Israel since 1970, and had been without work since his application. The Slepaks had briefly hung a banner from their Moscow apartment balcony, saying, "Let us join our son in Israel." Mrs. Slepak's case was separated from her husband's because she was in the hospital with a bleeding ulcer.

· Ida Nudel, 47-year-old economist, was convicted in a sepa-rate trial on the same charge as Slepak. She had been seeking permission to emigrate to Israel since 1971, and had also hung a sign from her balcony, saying "KGB, give me my visa."

· Yuri Orlov, a 53-year-old physicist who set up the first group to monitor the Soviet government's observance of human rights under the 1975 Helsinki accord on East-West coopera-tion, was sentenced to seven years in prison to be followed by five years in exile for the crime of "anti-Soviet agitation."

· Viktora Petkus, 49, translator of literature, was sentenced to ten years in prison to be followed by five years of internal exile. He was founder of a Helsinki watch group in Lithuania.

· Alexander Ginzburg, 41, found guilty of "anti-Soviet agita-tion and propaganda," was sentenced to eight years in a strict labor camp. A human rights advocate, he administered a fund (set up by royalties contributed by the writer Solzhenitsyn) to aid the families of political prisoners. This was his third prison sentence in the last 20 years.

· Anatoly B. Shcharansky, 30, computer specialist, a leader of the Jewish emigration movement, was sentenced to 13 years in prison and labor camps for treason, espionage, and anti-Soviet agitation.

If we get a little closer to the Orlov case, we can see in it an example of how dissent is born and the course it takes. Orlov was a member of the Communist Party in 1956, when Khrushchev denounced the terror under Stalin. At a party meeting the young physicist called for full de-Stalinization, which would not merely expose the dead dictator's crimes but would bring to justice those who carried out his orders. But Communist officials wanted to contain the potentially explosive effect of the Khrushchev speech and Orlov was expelled from the party for going too far. He lost his post at the Institute of Theoretical and Experimental Physics in Moscow and went to Erivan in Armenia to find work. There he became active for human rights. After reading the Helsinki Agreement, in which the U.S.S.R., the United States, and thirty-one other nations committed themselves to certain measures having to do with security, disarmament, trade, and also the observance of human rights, Orlov took the lead in forming the Helsinki Watch Group. Its aim was to investigate and report on how well his government lived up to those guarantees of human rights. There was nothing illegal about the group. True, it was unofficial, but clearly permissible, even called for by the Helsinki Final Act.

Orlov's group distributed reports to the embassies of all the Helsinki signers as well as to foreign correspondents. As foreign radio stations broadcast back into the Soviet Union the Watch Group's reports, dissidents elsewhere organized similar committees. Groups sprang up in Kiev, Vilnius, Erivan, Tiflis.

Sensitive to all facets of dissidence, the intensely committed Orlov was able to persuade disaffected people to put aside their differences. He introduced Georgian nationalists who wanted to secede to Jews who wanted to emigrate, and they formed watch groups, too. He encouraged Christians who wanted freedom to worship and artists who wanted freedom to paint to publicize their grievances. Dissidents who had rarely worked together before now found common ground.

Orlov was evidently too effective a dissenter for the government to tolerate. It began to move against the Helsinki Watch Group early in 1977, arresting Alexander Ginzburg first, then Orlov a week later, and soon after, Anatoly Shcharansky. Members of Watch Groups in Georgia and the Ukraine were also arrested at this time. Ginzburg, a poet who had previously served two terms for anti-Soviet agitation, was managing a fund set aside by Solzhenitsyn to aid families of political prisoners. Shcharansky, a Jew whose profession is computer scientist, had applied in 1973 for an exit visa to emigrate to Israel. Although the right to emigrate, at least for the purpose of reuniting split families, is firmly declared in the Helsinki Agreement, he was fired from his job and became active in the human rights movement, joining the Watch Group when it started. He was one of the first people whose actions linked both the human rights movement and the movement of Jews and others who simply want to leave the country. Long after he was imprisoned, Shcharansky, accused of working for U.S. intelligence, was charged with treason, which carries a potential death sentence.

Orlov was kept in prison, incommunicado, for fifteen months before standing trial in May 1978. The trial was held in a small courthouse in Moscow, sealed off from the public by the police.

Aside from a hostile crowd of spectators bussed in to pack the court, no one was allowed to enter the courtroom except Orlov's wife and two sons. (It was the first time she had been permitted to see her husband since his arrest.) The police kept out an American diplomat who wished to observe the trial, the Western reporters, and all of Orlov's friends and supporters, including Andrei Sakharov. Orlov's family said, that in defense of his actions, he contended he had the right to criticize the government and, under the freedom of information provisions of the Helsinki accord, to circulate such criticism. He did so not for subversive ends but out of concern for human rights.

Soviet law calls for open trials, but the authorities even prevented attempts to record detailed accounts of the court's proceedings. Mrs. Orlov was ordered not to take notes, and tape recorders her sons brought in were taken away. Mrs. Orlov made notes anyway, but when she left the courtroom she was forcibly searched and the notes confiscated.

Orlov asked that eleven witnesses be called in his behalf, but the judge declined to allow their appearance. A British lawyer had been engaged to defend him, but the authorities barred him from entering the Soviet Union.

Fifteen witnesses were called by the state to testify against Orlov. Under Soviet law, conviction on the charge of "anti-Soviet agitation and propaganda" requires showing that statements made do not correspond with reality. What the witnesses said aimed to show that reports issued by Orlov's group monitoring violations of human rights were false, and that Soviet society was free, democratic, and decent. Orlov was denied permission to examine documents in evidence and he was not given the chance to conduct full cross-examination of prosecution witnesses.

As the prosecutor made his summation and asked for the maximum sentence, the hand-picked spectators in the court-room shouted at Orlov, "Traitor!," "Spy!," and "Supporter of war!" When the sentence was read—it was the maximum allowed, seven years in prison followed by five years of exile—the spectators yelled, "He should have been given more!"

Judging by Orlov's case, it can be seen that in political trials the Soviet state does not observe in fact the legal standards that exist on paper. The Soviet constitution says, "Proceedings in all courts shall be open to the public." And another article reads, "Persecution for criticism is prohibited." As for what Orlov was doing that caused his arrest, did not the Soviet Union, in signing the Helsinki accord, promise with thirty-two other nations to "recognize the universal significance of human rights and fundamental freedoms, respect for which is an essential factor for the peace, justice and well-being neces-sary to ensure the development of friendly relations and co-operating among themselves"?

One of the more famous Soviet prisoners of conscience was Vladimir Bukovsky, who was released from prison in 1976, in an unprecedented exchange for another prisoner, Chile's Com-munist leader, Luis Corvalán. Born in 1942, Bukovsky was expelled from high school and then from college for the offense of creating or circulating samizdat literature. At twenty he was arrested and charged with possessing two photo-copies of a banned book, Milovan Djilas's *The New Class*. A commis-sion of psychiatrists examined him and declared him not accountable for his actions. He was sent to the Leningrad prison psychiatric hospital—"15 months of hell," he called it —and, when released, he helped plan a demonstration in sup-port of the writers Andrei Sinyavsky and Yuli Daniel, who had been arrested for permitting their nonconformist works to be published abroad. But before this happened, Bukovsky was again committed to a madhouse, this time for eight months. About a year later he was arrested a third time, for organizing a demonstration protesting the arrests of four fellow dissidents. This time he was shipped to a labor camp for three years. Released in 1970, he said in an interview broadcast abroad:

> The essence of the struggle, in my view, is the struggle against fear—the fear which has gripped the people since Stalin's time and which still has not left them, and thanks to which the system continues to exist—the system of dictatorship, of pressure, of oppression. It is into this struggle against fear that we put our greatest efforts, and in that struggle great importance attaches to personal example, the example which we give people.
>
> I personally did what I considered right, spoke out on those occasions when I wanted to, and I'm alive. I am now sitting here and not in prison. I'm alive, I can get about, I can live. For me and for my people that is very important—it shows that it is possible to fight, and that it is necessary.

What Bukovsky did now was the unforgivable: he acquired the forensic psychiatric diagnoses of six dissenters being held in mental hospitals and sent them to the West. An accompanying letter cited the confinement cases of many such people known for their action in defense of human rights. With the copies of the official documents he sent letters and other material characterizing those confined and asked the Western experts to reach their own conclusions about the dissenters' mental condition. The texts of these expert findings were published in Washington in 1972, under the title *Abuse of Psychiatry for Political Repression in the Soviet Union*.

Bukovsky's defense of those forced illegally into psychiatric confinement resulted in his arrest once again, on charges of anti-Soviet propaganda. In his final plea to the court, he said:

> By my trial, the regime is striving to conceal its own crimes— psychiatric reprisals against dissidents.
>
> Their reprisals against me are an attempt to frighten those who are trying to tell the world about their crimes. They want to avoid "washing their dirty linen in public" so that they can appear, in the world arena, as irreproachable defenders of the oppressed!
>
> Our society is sick. It is sick with the fear we inherited from the time of Stalin's terror. But the process of society's spiritual regeneration has already begun, and there is no stopping it. And society already understands that the criminal is not the person who washes dirty linen in public, but the person who dirties the linen in the first place. And for whatever length of time that I have to stay in prison, I will never renounce my convictions. I will express them, taking advantage of the right guaranteed me by Article 125 of the Soviet Constitution, to everyone who is willing to listen to me. I will fight for legality and justice.

He was sentenced to twelve years. He was then twenty-nine. From the first day he reached Perm prison camp 35 in the Ural Mountains, Bukovsky was singled out for the harshest treatment; his canteen privileges were denied, his mother's visits canceled, he was confined to punishment cells. To protest cruel and arbitrary treatment of the prisoners, he organized hunger strikes in the camp, one of which lasted a month.

While in prison camp Bukovsky managed the impossible. He met a fellow prisoner, Dr. Semyon Gluzman, a young psychiatrist from Kiev sentenced to seven years for anti-Soviet propaganda. Gluzman, too, had denounced the political corruption of his own profession in a samizdat document, analyzing as an example the fraudulent diagnosis of General Pyotr Grigorenko, who had spent years in solitary confinement in a psychoprison. Although under constant surveillance in the camp, Bukovsky and Gluzman succeeded in discussing their ideas on how to combat the abuse, composed *A Manual on Psychiatry for Dissidents*, and had it smuggled out to the West, where it was published in London.

The first paragraphs of the manual expose the insidious nature of this technique of political repression:

It is well known that in the Soviet Union today large numbers of dissidents are being declared insane, and there is reason to fear that this method will be used on an even greater scale in the future. It is not difficult to find an explanation for this phenomenon. From the point of view of the authorities, it is an extremely convenient method: it enables them to deprive a man of his freedom for an unlimited length of time, keep him in strict isolation, and use psycho-pharmacological means of "re-educating" him; it hinders the campaign for open legal proceedings and for his release, since even the most impartial man will, if he is not personally acquainted with the patient, always feel a twinge of uncertainty about the patient's mental health; it deprives its victim of what few rights he would enjoy as a prisoner, and it provides an opportunity to discredit the ideas and actions of dissidents, etc., etc.

There is, however, another, no less important side. Dissidents, as a rule, have enough legal grounding so as not to make mistakes during their investigation and trials, but when confronted by a qualified psychiatrist with a directive from above to have them declared non-accountable, they have found themselves absolutely powerless. All this has, inevitably, engendered re-

newed fear and dismay in dissident circles and is the reason for
cases of unexpected "repentance" and renunciation which have
occurred in recent months. Forensic psychiatry has thus renewed
the fear of persecution, which a knowledge of the law and skill
in applying it had previously dispelled. A mood of resignation
to one's fate, a sense of one's powerlessness to resist this
method of persecution, has become widespread.

But what happens when a dissident is diagnosed as schizo-
phrenic, the usual label applied? Dr. Walter Reich, an American psychiatrist who has made a close study of the Soviet
technique, puts it this way:

> The diagnosed dissident is put on trial, a trial that may be held
> without him because he is considered too sick to attend; the
> judges almost always accept the psychiatrists' diagnosis and
> finding of non-responsibility; and the dissident is sent not to a
> prison or labor camp but to a psychiatric hospital, usually of
> a "special," high-security type, one designed to hold the
> criminally insane . . .
> What is accomplished by all this is that dissenting views are
> pronounced the sick products of sick minds; dissidents are de-
> prived of the opportunity to defend themselves at open trials;
> and, without being given definite sentences that end after, say,
> three to seven years, they are sent to hospitals until they are
> pronounced well, a judgment that may not be made until the
> KGB decides they are well. Finally, should they ever dissent
> again, that dissent may be considered a sign of the recurrence
> of their lifelong disease.

After his collaboration with Gluzman, Bukovsky was transferred to the dread Vladimir prison, where he continued his

defense of the rights of fellow prisoners. By 1975, in addition to rheumatic heart disease contracted in earlier confinements, he had come down with a liver disease, a duodenal ulcer, and an eye ailment. His extraordinary example of courage brought international appeals for his freedom. It came finally, at the end of 1976.

Bukovsky's campaign against the abuse of psychiatry, joined by many others in the Soviet Union and outside, finally led the World Psychiatric Association (WPA) at its Hawaii meeting in 1977 to adopt three resolutions. One created an international code of ethics for psychiatrists and barred the internment in psychiatric hospitals of people who are not mentally ill. Another condemned the political use of psychiatry wherever it occurs, but singled out the U.S.S.R. for censure because it was abundantly proved that abuses occurred there. The third resolution authorized the creation of a permanent commission of inquiry within the WPA to investigate abuses of psychiatry for political purposes.

Is the Soviet Union the only country where such abuse of psychiatry occurs? Argentina, Chile, East Germany, Romania, and South Africa have been alleged to use psychiatrists as adjuncts of the secret police in the state's system of political repression.

One of the main tributaries to the broad streams of dissent is the movement for religious freedom. Religious dissent bothers the government even more than the better-publicized manifestoes of the intellectuals because this growing movement is shaped by ordinary people at the grass roots. As early as 1961, the Evangelical Christians and the Baptists began to organize in resistance to a new wave of antireligious persecution. When the Soviet authorities tried to suppress the movement by jailing hundreds of its activists, their families established a Council of Prisoners' Relatives. It protested the steady erosion of qualified religious freedom guaranteed in early Soviet law. Soon Pentecostals, Russian Orthodox Church reformers, Seventh-Day Adventists added their voices to the Baptists in the struggle for religious liberty. The Helsinki Watch Group took up such religious issues as the treatment of Adventist families, particularly the deprivation of parental rights and the removal of children to boarding schools. Non-Christian dissidents and Christians of all denominations were drawn together, through common suffering, in the daily battle for their rights.

The Jewish emigration movement, of course, is another voice in the dissident chorus. It was in 1963 that Soviet Jews began to demand cultural and religious rights for themselves equal to those of all the Soviet nationalities. They protested denial of facilities for Yiddish culture, the forced closing of synagogues, the absence of legal means for educating their children in the Jewish religion and the Hebrew language, and the open anti-Semitism permitted and often encouraged by the authorities. But not until after the Israeli victory in the 1967 Six-Day War did large numbers of Soviet Jews join the movement for their rights. What began as a struggle for parity became a movement for the right to emigrate to Israel. Perhaps in the hope of obtaining Western economic aid and technology, the Soviet Union permitted some emigration while trying to dampen enthusiasm for more changes.

Jews in the Soviet Union have many reasons for wishing to leave. There are the Zionists, who want to live in Israel. There are non-Zionist Jews, who simply wish to join relatives in other countries. Other Jews wish to pursue academic, scientific, or literary careers in countries where there is neither anti-Semitism nor government censorship. And finally, there are those who out of total rejection of all things Soviet would go anywhere, no matter what the place or the consequences. The campaign for emigration, aided by sympathetic pressure from the West, brought about the departure of over 150,000 Jews by early 1978. This is only a small fraction of Soviet Jewry, it should be noted, for 2.5 million still remain. Yet it is an amazing accomplishment, when one recalls how rigid was the barrier to emigration up to the 1960s.

To emigrate, an exit visa is needed, for which some form of documentary evidence of Jewish origin is demanded. An invitation from a relative of the applicant to join him in Israel is commonly asked for. The submission of such an invitation is no guarantee of a visa. The unlucky applicant may be refused, often on grounds of having had access to "classified" information. These "refuseniks," as they are called, are then subjected to official harassment. Many have lost their jobs or been expelled from school. Some have had trouble even getting medical care. They become marked people. Colleagues and friends are afraid to associate with them. Sometimes they are left dangling, with no action on a visa taken one way or another. Those fired from their posts are effectively prevented from getting work elsewhere. They may then be charged with the Soviet crime of "parasitism" and sent to prison or a labor camp, or into exile in Siberia. To stubbornly and publicly persist in the struggle for the right to emigrate risks punishment for the crime of "hooliganism."

A special target of repression is nationalism in the federated republics which are components of the Soviet Union. The best-known example, perhaps, is that of the Ukraine, the second most populous Soviet republic. It now has some 50 million people living on a territory a bit bigger than France. Its independent history and culture go back to the early Middle Ages. A dependency of the Russian empire since 1654, it has long resisted attempts by czar or commissar to wipe out its culture and language. In the early 1960s young Ukrainian intellectuals fostered a dramatic renaissance of national identity and self-respect. When the old charges of "anti-Soviet propaganda" and "bourgeois nationalism" were raised against the dissident literature which deplored the Ukraine's colonial status and the stunting of its culture, young Ukrainians appealed to the Soviet Constitution and the UN Universal Declaration of Human Rights. Scores were arrested for their criticism and sent to prison camps. One of the boldest spokesmen to emerge in the 1960s was Valentyn Moroz, a Ukrainian historian, the son of peasants. By 1977, at the age of forty, he had spent all but nine months of the previous decade in prison for "thought crimes." Stricken with liver and blood ailments, he had nevertheless carried out a 145-day hunger strike to protest against conditions in the notorious Vladimir prison, near Moscow. His chief crime was to oppose abuse of power, especially the Soviet regime's nationalities policy, which he termed lightly veiled Russification and cultural genocide. The essays he wrote in prison are brilliant examples of samizdat. In one of them he speaks of Soviet society as an "empire of cogs," produced on the assembly line by fanatical bureaucrats:

> The cog is the cherished idea of any totalizator. An obedient herd of cogs can be called a parliament or an academic council, and you will have no trouble or surprises from it. A cog called a professor or an academician will never say anything new, and

if it does produce a surprise, it will do so not by new words, but by the lightning-swift change of its conceptions. A herd of cogs can be termed the Red Cross, and it will count calories in Africa but say not a single word about famine at home. A cog will emerge from prison and immediately write that it was never there, and what is more, will call the person who demanded its release a liar. A cog will shoot at whomever it is told to and then, on command, campaign for peace. The final and most important advantage is that once people have been turned into cogs, you can blithely introduce any constitution you want to, give them the right to anything. The exquisite point is that it will never enter a cog's head to wield this right.

Fiercely resentful of Russian domination, other national groups have been increasingly militant in their attempts to protect their cultural integrity and their dignity as a people. Mass demonstrations involving as many as five to twelve thousand people have taken place on the city streets of Georgia. In the Soviet republics of Georgia and Armenia, popular outcry succeeded recently in preventing plans to drop Georgian and Armenian as the official state languages.

The growing assertiveness of non-Russian ethnic groups has its counterpart in an intensified Russian nationalism. The voices of such Russian nationalists are also heard among the dissidents. None of them speaks for democratic values in the Western sense. The most conspicuous and apparently popular nationalists believe in the superiority of Russianness and in the inferiority of all things non-Russian. They think the Soviet Union has been corrupted by everything "foreign"—liberal reforms, Western products, intellectuals, Jews, moves toward détente. They want to strengthen the most conservative and authoritarian elements in Soviet political life. Their samizdat writings echo the racism, the anti-Semitism, the militarism of the Nazis. Their drift is back to a Russia of the czarist days or of Stalinism.

For advocates of human rights, the freedom to criticize, to speak up, to be heard, is a value to be cherished and fought for. But while supporting the right to dissent, one does not necessarily endorse the ideas of every dissenter.

7

Torture—the Ultimate Corruption

TORTURE—the word has a special horror for most of us, because we know pain, and we fear it even more intensely when we think of one human being deliberately inflicting pain upon another in order to break him. In each of the countries discussed thus far, torture has been mentioned as a tool used by the state to maintain its power.

But not only in these few states. In *Report on Torture*, issued by Amnesty International in 1975, sufficient evidence was gathered to document the use of torture in at least sixty countries. (That number would have been greater if AI had been able to gather the proofs it insists upon before accepting allegations of torture.) The AI report concludes that torture "is indeed a world-wide phenomenon that does not belong solely to one political ideology or to one economic system . . . The torture of citizens regardless of sex, age, or state of health in an effort to retain political power is a practice encouraged by some governments and tolerated by others in an increasingly large number of countries . . . What for the last two or three hundred years has been no more than a historical curiosity has suddenly developed a life of its own and become a social cancer."

Next to murder, torture is the most terrible violation of human rights one person can inflict upon another. Like murder, the practice is as old as mankind. History teaches us the human capacity for torture. Ingenious men devised innumerable means of inflicting physical and mental pain to get evidence or a confession. Ancient Egypt employed torture, and so, of course, did the Greeks and the Romans. It was used widely in the Middle Ages. During the Inquisition the Catholic Church racked, scourged, or burned suspected heretics to make them recant. When Elizabeth I took the throne and restored the Church of England, she sent Jesuit priests to the Tower to be tortured. If the state could torture the common criminal, why couldn't the rack and the thumbscrew be used against the more serious crime of heresy?

With the Enlightenment, torture lost its official sanction in many nations. The French Declaration of the Rights of Man set a high standard for a new age by abolishing torture "forever." Slavemasters, of course, continued to rely on the lash, mutilation, and branding. Torture accompanied European imperialists to the lands of Africa, Asia, and the New World. Still, by the early twentieth century, scholars could write optimistically that the barbarous practice was gone, or at least vanishing, from this civilized earth—only to discover, with the rise of Communism and Fascism, that ideology was replacing religion as the driving force for persecution. The masters of the new regimes would include torture among their instruments of repression and intimidation.

One of the few directives that have come to light from a head of government approving the use of torture is a coded telegram from Stalin to the head of the NKVD, the Soviet secret police (now known as the KGB). Dated January 20, 1939, it reads in part: "The Party Central Committee explains that application of methods of physical pressure in NKVD practice is permissible from 1937 on, in accordance with permission of the Party Central Committee . . . It is known that all bourgeois intelligence services use methods of physical influence against the representatives of socialist proletariat and that they use them in the most scandalous forms. The question arises as to why the socialist intelligence service should be more humanitarian against the mad agents of the bourgeoisie, against the deadly enemies of the working class and of the collective farm workers. The Party Central Committee considers that physical pressure should still be used obligatorily, as an exception applicable to known and obstinate enemies of the people, as a method both justifiable and appropriate."

The text was disclosed in Khrushchev's secret speech to the Twentieth Party Congress in Moscow in 1956. The implication was that, from then on, the crimes committed under Stalin, including the "barbaric torture . . . mass arrests and deportations . . . executions without trial . . ." would cease.

Of Hitler's use of torture there is no end of evidence. The Nazi apparatus of terror was merciless. Objections to what went on in the torture chambers were dismissed on the ground that the victims were only "animals" or "criminals." The Nazi concentration camps (like the Soviet camps which preceded them) were used to eliminate every form of active or potential opposition. The Nazis beat, flayed, strangled, shot, and gassed their victims. The aim always was to rob prisoners first of their dignity and humanity. The progressive terror Hitler launched against the Jews as soon as his hand grasped the lever of power ended only with the extermination of 6 million in the death camps.

The 1948 UN Declaration of Human Rights condemning torture was a response to the universal revulsion against Hitler's crimes. But torture did not stop. In Algeria, in Northern Ireland, in Greece, in Vietnam, wherever there have been colonial, civil, or territorial wars, insurrection or terrorism, torture has continued. Worse, it has been made an administrative policy of the modern state. No longer the exception, it is the rule in scores of nations. Today authoritarian states use torture as a means of governing.

Everywhere the motives are the same: to obtain confession of personal guilt, to get evidence of the guilt of others, to break the human spirit, to force unquestioned obedience, to intimidate potential dissenters.

Does torture work? Beccaria, the Italian jurist, wrote in 1764: "The strength of the muscles and the sensitivity of the nerves of an innocent person being known factors, the problem is to find the level of suffering necessary to make him confess to any given crime." This has rarely been a problem in the past, even with the crudest instruments. Today, with sophisticated technology, the torturers can destroy the will of almost anybody. Of course, torture can produce false confessions and wrong information and is therefore inefficient. It is also inefficient because there are better, more intelligent ways to get information. But such arguments imply that if torture *were* efficient, its use would be justified.

No, the argument against torture is essentially a moral one. "Torture is never justified," concludes the AI report. "The absolute prohibition on torture is the only acceptable policy. The system that uses it only mocks any noble ends it might profess . . . Man with his innate aggression has learned to place limits on his capacity for excess. He has learned to place limits on the exercise of the power by the few to protect the many and ultimately to protect everyone. Torture is the most flagrant denial of man's humanity, it is the ultimate human corruption. For this reason man has prohibited it."

A prohibition ignored in much of the world . . . In Latin America, where police brutality has long been traditional, systematic torture in the last decade has become a standard practice of the new military regimes. From every country in Latin America but Costa Rica, AI received allegations of torture in a single year. The governments have paid only lip service to their own constitutional bans on torture and to the safeguards against it agreed upon by the Organization of American States (OAS).

Uruguay, for instance, once highly regarded as an advanced and stable democracy, was seized by a military junta in 1972. It swiftly banned all political parties, unions, and student groups. In 1978 the Inter-American Commission on Human Rights, an autonomous agency of the OAS, issued a report charging the Uruguay regime with wholesale violations of human rights, including arbitrary arrest, torture, and murder of political prisoners. So many people were thrown into jail that on a per capita basis Uruguay could boast the largest concentration of political prisoners of any country in the world—one for every 450 citizens. The commission produced evidence that torture methods used by the Uruguay military and police included beatings of all types, electric prods to sensitive parts of the body, repeated immersions upside down in a tank of water mixed with vomit, blood, or urine, and sexual acts of violence.

One could select almost at random variations on these methods from what is already an appallingly voluminous documentary literature of torture. Take the case of Luis Armando Guzman Luna, a student in Nicaragua. He "disappeared" after detention by the National Guard one day in 1975. Not until some three months later was he brought before a military court as a "witness." Numerous sources reported he had been tortured in prison. A document prepared by prisoners described his treatment:

> Nine consecutive days torture: punches, kicks, beating with gun butts, beating with sticks on shins and elbows, neck and head, electric shocks, nine days standing up, and eight days without food and drinking water, kicks in the testicles, 95 days incommunicado and hooded.

Evidence of torture in Greece and Chile was gathered by a Danish Medical Group organized in 1974 to help Amnesty International in its campaign against torture. Among the group's several studies is one combining findings made by examining thirty-two Chilean political prisoners who found refuge in Denmark and thirty-five Greek political prisoners the doctors examined in Greece after the fall of the fascist Junta.

First, here is a list of the methods of torture used on the prisoners in Chile and Greece:

Beating

Direct cranial trauma

Falanga (continual flogging on the soles of the feet)

Electrical torture

Sleep deprivation

Solitary confinement

Starvation and dehydration

Sexual exploitation

Direct genital trauma

Threatening of family and friends

Enforced witnessing or overhearing torture of others

Threats of execution

Pharmacological torture

Tooth torture

Suspension by feet or hands

Water torture

Bright light torture

Other forms of torture

"Virtually all the victims had been beaten," said the medical report, "and in two-thirds of the cases, the beating had included trauma to the head. *Falanga* was inflicted only on the Greek prisoners: 29 of the 35. Electrical torture involved placing electrodes on any part of the body, particularly the head (ears, nose and mouth), and the genitalia . . . Sexual violation was rare in both groups, but beating of the genitalia common. Eighteen of the Chileans and 20 of the Greeks were tortured in other ways as well: they were threatened with execution, burnt with cigarettes, deprived of sleep, kept standing over long periods, had their nails torn out, submerged in excrement and buried alive, then disinterred . . ."

It's worth noting that in many countries physicians have collaborated in torture. They have helped plan torture, both in deciding how much the individual can tolerate and in refining torture methods so as to prevent the appearance of physical symptoms that could be used as evidence of the infliction of torture.

Everyone knows now how in the name of "medical science" the Nazis made special use of the doomed Jews. These "experiments"—many of them having nothing to do with healing the sick but with "improved" methods of killing—numbered their victims in the hundreds of thousands. German physicians collaborated in such torture, as well as in carrying out brutal assignments at Auschwitz and the other death camps.

There are many refinements on torture that medical and other scientists have introduced, using advances in physical and psychological research to go beyond the cruder, old-fashioned techniques. One of modern technology's contributions, for instance, is what the torturers call the "refrigerator." It's a five-foot cube containing loudspeakers, strobe lights, and heating and cooling units. The victim is bombarded with sensory stimuli ranging from fiery heat to extreme cold, from terrible noise to total silence, and from bright light to darkness. Nervous collapse and capitulation is the almost inevitable result. Another gadget is a vest which can be inflated to increase pressure on the chest during interrogation, sometimes crushing the rib cage.

Drugs are widely used by torturers to cause suffering. Some drugs, such as LSD, disrupt the normal perceptual and conceptual processes and will confuse, distress, and weaken the victim. Other drugs are used to induce such unpleasant sensations that the victim is filled with dread. In the Soviet Union, where it has been a practice to declare many dissidents insane and lock them up for years in prison psychiatric hospitals, drug treatments produce pain and suffering as acute as more physical methods of torture.

One of the worst examples of drug misuse in the Soviet Union is the case of Leonid Plyushch. A twenty-eight-year-old mathematician working in a cybernetics institute, he was dismissed in 1968 for criticizing a newspaper article about a political trial. A year later he became a founder of the Action Group for the Defense of Human Rights. Despite pressure on him to quit his dissent, he persisted in it. In 1972 he was arrested and after eighteen months' detention was put in a Special Psychiatric Hospital on the recommendation of a psychiatric commission. He was held there two-and-a-half years. Within three months drug damage to a perfectly normal man had so transformed him physically and mentally his wife could hardly recognize him. He was savagely dosed, not only to punish him, but to destroy him as a dissenter and as a human being. Later, after release, he said of the drugs' effect upon him:

> I saw in my own case that the first days are meant to break a person morally straight away, break down his will to fight. Then begins the "treatment" with tranquilizers. I was horrified to see how I deteriorated intellectually, morally and emotionally from day to day. My interest in political problems quickly disappeared, then my interest in scientific problems, and then my interest in my wife and children. This was replaced by fear for my wife and children. My speech became jerky and abrupt. My memory also deteriorated.

Because a powerful protest was mounted against the mistreatment of Plyushch, both in the Soviet Union and abroad, the regime probably chose to use maximum brutality in defiance of the human rights movement. But the negative wave of publicity rose so high, the release of Plyushch was finally ordered. He now lives in France.

One of the hardest aspects of being sent to a psychoprison is the indefinite term of the confinement. There is no appeal; one could remain there for the rest of one's life. Stripped of every right, defenseless, alone, there is only one way to obtain release—renouncing one's convictions. One must say officially to the doctors (which means to the state), "I was sick, I didn't know what I was doing, I won't do it again." People with the integrity and courage of a Grigorenko or a Plyushch find it impossible to recant.

The Soviet Union, since Khrushchev's 1956 speech, has never again admitted to the practice of torture. On the other hand, after thirty years in power, Communist China began in 1978 to publicize abuses of its citizens' rights, promising to correct them. When a decade of turmoil ended soon after the death of Mao Tse-tung, the Communist leadership began to introduce new policies designed to modernize the economy and to give the people a better and more open life. As wall posters (China's form of samizdat) appeared, demanding more democracy, prominent party leaders exposed the existence of political persecution of innocent people. The Chinese press carried accounts of widespread arbitrary detention and illegal methods of investigation, including torture. Even China's own Ministry of Public Security published a lengthy report acknowledging torture and other abuses. Thousands of innocent workers and students had suffered detention, arrest, and isolation. One example given was of a performer detained and tortured after she wrote a letter complaining of nepotism in her opera company. Another case reported was of an electrical engineer who died as a result of brutal interrogation methods. Hsinhua, the official press agency, disclosed that in Shanghai ten thousand scientists, along with members of their families, had been falsely accused of being agents of the old Nationalist regime during the Cultural Revolution and subjected to mental and physical torture. The sixty-seven-year-old former mayor of Shanghai was tortured to death by radicals in 1976. When the principal Peking daily, *Jenmin Jih Pao*, began to publish a new column of complaints from readers, it received over 130,000 letters in five months detailing experiences of corruption and persecution. Proof of how common such experiences were came when the government released about 100,000 people who had been held in jail as rightists since 1957.

The first spontaneous political demonstrations held in China since the Communists took power in 1949 brought out thousands in late 1978; they called for freedom and democracy. But it remains to be seen whether totalitarianism in China and large-scale violation of human rights are coming to an end. Some scholars of Chinese history think it naïve to expect that a China with a 2,000-year-old tradition of centralized authoritarian rule will transform itself into a political democracy in the Western sense. The primary aims of the post-Mao leadership are to speed up scientific, technological, and industrial development so as to modernize the country. To achieve these goals they must mobilize the energy and talent of their nearly one billion people. That requires encouraging a freer expression of opinion, but as the Communists see it, within definite boundaries. What China needs now, its leaders are saying, is "stability, unity, discipline." A new legal system to prevent future political persecution and some genuine elections of officials are being urged. But is it likely that anything that would weaken the legitimacy of the regime or threaten the position of its leaders will be tolerated?

In another Communist regime, Cambodia, ruled by the Khmer Rouge from April 1975 until the Vietnamese army overthrew it in January 1979, self-imposed isolation from the outside world made the gathering of evidence on torture extremely difficult. Nevertheless, reports by many refugees and by a group of Yugoslav journalists (Communists) allowed to make a tour indicated that Cambodians suffered almost total violation of human rights. The country seemed to be "a vast and somber work camp" where toil was unending, rewards nonexistent, families separated, and murder "a constantly used tool of social discipline."

Bloodletting in Cambodia continued for years, accompanied by mass starvation and nationwide forced labor. The principal targets for extermination were the educated, officials down to the most minor in previous governments, and former soldiers of the pre-1975 army and their families. Growing numbers of local Communist officials, too, were killed in factional purges. The detailed reports of Communist atrocities were horrifying. Murder and the threat of murder as a means of control were the ultimate forms of torture. Students of Cambodia, a land of 7 million people, believed that over 1.2 million Cambodians died as a result of Communist rule. It was a case of genocide by the regime against its own people.

In Africa, the colonial powers relied on torture to keep down nationalist movements. During their long struggle for freedom, activists in the liberation movements were often the victims of brutality. In those few African countries still dominated by white minority regimes, the use of torture against the African majority has been exposed time and again by international investigations. But since liberation, most of the new African states, according to the AI's *Report on Torture*, have themselves employed torture against internal political dissidents or to suppress religious or racial groups. This despite the fact that most of their constitutions guarantee protection against torture. At times torture has been used by the military against civilians, and at other times by civilians against civilians of differing ethnic backgrounds. Torture has also been used to force confessions or extract evidence not only in political but in common law trials.

Uganda is only the worst example of an African state where torture was made an administrative practice. After the army coup of 1971, which put Idi Amin in power, torture, mutilation, and massacre were applied on a vastly greater scale than under Amin's predecessor, Obote. In a country riven by tribal dissension, Amin was accused of carrying out tribal massacres. Both soldiers and civilians suspected of dissension were flogged or mutilated until they were dead. British journalists detained briefly in one of Amin's military prisons witnessed floggings and beatings with rifle butts and learned from other prisoners that African prisoners had been forced by Ugandan soldiers to smash each other's skull with hammers. High officials fallen out of favor were brutally tortured prior to execution. One list, compiled by Henry Kyemba, a former minister in the Amin government, shows over a hundred ambassadors, ministers, physicians, religious leaders, and professors murdered by Amin's private assassination squads. Amin's wildly unpredictable, random methods of killing cost the lives of over 100,000 Ugandans. Not until 1979 was Amin finally deposed by Tanzanian troops allied with Ugandan exiles.

Can anything be done about torture? Ramsey Clark, a former U.S. Attorney General, says:

> To debate seriously the necessity or desirability of torture is to expose an absence of human values. To justify it in the name of realism, practicality and survival encourages the deadly game. To call for torture in the defense of freedom mocks freedom. People so insensitive to the nature of freedom as to invoke torture in its defense have already lost their freedom.
>
> Torture must be unthinkable. Once resistance to the idea of torture is eroded, its use will spread. The notion that there are evil or dangerous people and that torture can be limited to them is contrary to history, experience and human nature. Once it is justified, those who merely oppose or threaten the authorities will suffer it.
>
> The abolition of torture is as important as the abolition of slavery. Torture is the cruelest effort to enslave and the most damaging. It must be prohibited absolutely . . .
>
> Universal outrage at the slightest suggestion that torture is acceptable is the one condition that can ultimately prevent torture . . . No law will significantly deter governments or their citizens from habits and hatreds unless there is a passionate commitment from the people in opposition to torture.

In 1975 the UN adopted a Declaration on the Protection of All Persons from Torture and Other Cruel, Inhuman or Degrading Treatment or Punishment (see Appendix). Two international organizations, the World Medical Association and the Council for International Organizations of the Medical Sciences, are trying to sensitize physicians throughout the world by preparing a Medical Code of Ethics relating to torture. AI, which has been sending investigative teams to police states or elsewhere to gather the evidence of torture, held a medical seminar on torture in Athens, Greece, in 1978. Out of the many medical, psychological, and other research reports given at Athens will come a case book on the effects of torture which could be used whenever and wherever legal redress is possible. AI's medical group is now recommending that an autopsy be performed by nongovernmental pathologists of all persons dying in prison.

8

The Power of the Word

It is not surprising . . . that art should be the enemy marked out by every form of oppression. It is not surprising that artists and intellectuals should have been the first victims of modern tyrannies, whether of the Left or the Right. Tyrants know that there is in the work of art an emancipatory force, which is mysterious only to those who do not revere it.

ALBERT CAMUS

Hardly a day passes without news of the silencing of some writer by an authoritarian regime. In just one year, 1977, the literary organization known as the PEN American Center recorded 606 cases of repression of writers in 55 countries. The writers worked in every form and in every medium. Most of them had been imprisoned, some were placed in psychiatric confinement, some sentenced to internal exile, and a few put under house arrest or under other severe restrictions. Many had been detained without charge or trial, often incommunicado. Any such list is incomplete, of course, for in totalitarian societies information on arrest and imprisonment is most difficult to obtain.

This, though freedom of thought and expression is one of the most elementary human rights. If citizens cannot voice their opinions without fear, then there is no way for them to shape the decisions of the state, to elect its officials, or to correct its mistakes. "Every government needs to know what its citizens think," wrote Akim Djilas, "the difference being in the methods it uses to find out: whether by allowing its citizens to express themselves freely, or by using the secret police to discover it." Djilas was reminding the Central Committee of the Yugoslav Communist Party of a simple fact.

Looking at it from a slightly different angle, the American journalist I. F. Stone said, "A society in which men are not free to speak their minds is not a good society, no matter what material benefits it may offer the few or the many. The only absolute value I would affirm is freedom of the mind—without it there cannot be social justice."

Writers in societies blighted by the totalitarian state feel it their moral duty to act as guide and conscience of their people. That is why so many of them spend months, years, and even much of their lives in prison. The South Korean poet and playwright Kim Chi Ha was sentenced to life imprisonment by the Park Chung Hee regime. Why? Because while sitting in prison on another charge (lampooning Park's despotic regime in verse), he had made notes for a literary work which the secret police confiscated and interpreted as proof that he was a Communist. At the time of this writing, he had been kept in a solitary confinement cell for three years, denied visits from family and lawyer, and forbidden writing materials and all reading matter, including a Bible.

In Kenya, one of Africa's best-known novelists and playwrights was arrested early in 1978 and held incommunicado without trial. Ngugi Wa Thiong'o, forty, was head of the department of literature at Nairobi University. He was detained for reasons of "public security." His latest works, a novel and a play, were highly critical of what has happened to post-independent Kenya. When his growing indictment of Kenya society became apparent in his writing, Ngugi was asked if he feared trouble with the authorities. "No," he replied, "I have no such fears because I believe that criticism of our social institutions and structures is a very healthy thing . . . Society can move forward only through sincere, open and healthy criticism. If writers don't do this anywhere in the world they would be failing in their duty."

Under Kenyan law Ngugi could be held indefinitely. But a year after he was imprisoned Ngugi was freed with other political prisoners by Daniel Arap Moi, who succeeded Jomo Kenyatta as president of Kenya.

In the Philippines, martial law was declared by President Ferdinand E. Marcos in 1972, although he prefers the euphemism "constitutional authoritarianism." His government seems to specialize in putting writers in jail. When *New York Times* columnist John Leonard visited Manila in 1978, three out of four of the dozens of writers he met had been in jail. The government controls the radio and the universities and owns or controls the magazines and newspapers. Since the state of martial law began, only one novel has been published.

The Peruvian novelist Mario Vargas Llosa explains why writers in Latin America are so often political figures too:

Traditionally literature in Latin America has been an outlet for information as well as a whole body of social criticism that could never have been offered in other ways, because of rigid censorship and repression in countries with no free press or free political life. Where there were no congresses and no political parties functioning freely because of the dictatorial systems, literature has been the only forum in which some of the countries' real problems could be expressed. That situation has given the writer a certain political presence . . . There's a point of coincidence in the extreme right and the extreme left. To some small extent it's the way throughout the world, but I'd say it's widespread in Latin America. Both coincide in authoritarianism. Both are resolute in not listening to the adversary's reasons and in closing off all possibilities for dialogue. This form of mental schematism has done enormous harm to Latin America. Today, because the extreme right has control in the great majority of Latin American countries, what exists is an authoritarianism of the right, but the truth is that in large portions of the left there is an equivalent mentality.

Protests against such narrow-minded, one-party rule are voiced by writers all over the world. Late in 1977 the dissident Yugoslav writer Mihajlo Mihajlov was released from prison under a government amnesty that included 217 other political prisoners. For thirteen years the only place he could publicly speak to his compatriots was the courtroom; he had spent more than half that period in prison. Saying he was ready to return to jail rather than stop criticizing the regime, he addressed a plea to the Belgrade conference on European security and cooperation, urging it not to omit human rights in its final document. (It did.) Rights come *first*, he kept saying:

> Today it is clear to everyone that the persecution of Jews in Germany was not an "internal question" of the Third Reich, just as today's apartheid policy in South Africa is not. It is clear to everyone that discrimination and spiritual genocide against

the color of ideas, which exist in all one-party systems, whether they are associated with an international one-party center or are independent—is as inexcusable as the discrimination against *the color of the skin*. It is also clear that those rights that allegedly exist in totalitarian societies—the right to work, apartment, medical and social care—mean nothing without other human rights because these same rights are granted in all the world's prisons.

For the first time in history, the emphasis on individual human rights is given top priority—thus everything falls in its right place and creates a new division among states, blocs and systems. In that new division, all one-party Communist states fall naturally along the side of South American dictatorships or South Africa . . . Totalitarianism survives *only* because it, in the name of race, class, ideology, nation or state, destroys precisely those elementary, individual human rights noted in the Helsinki Agreement, most notably the right to free speech.

. . . I know the power of a free man's word, and I know that no state, monopoly, party or police can force one to renounce his right to speak, when one is prepared to back his words with all one possesses: freedom, material well-being and life itself . . .

Can there be a question of freedom of exchange of ideas and information where every spoken word or thought not in line with resolutions of the latest plenum of the monopolistic and almighty party is declared an *"ideological diversion"* and is persecuted in the same manner as the act of planting dynamite?

The pressures placed upon a writer in prison to recant are suggested by these paragraphs from a book by the Croatian poet Mirko Vidovic. He spent five years in Yugoslav prisons before being released as a result of diplomatic intervention by the French government:

All the time the prison authorities were tightening up their psychological pressures on me by informing me—through no less a person than the Reeducator-in-Chief—that I could only enjoy my long-awaited release if I were to change my attitude towards the current political situation in the country . . .

In prison they wanted to sell us the right to see our wives and children for a few minutes more, and the right to scribble a few more lines in our letters out. They sold us our own patience for the sake of a glimmer of hope, they promised us peace if we sold our souls to them—they in return sold us the possibility of finding work on leaving prison as long as we agreed to bear false witness . . .

There, among these human wrecks, they tried to accustom us little by little to the idea that we ourselves were in some way unhealthy or abnormal. They wanted us to lose our identity so that our brains could function as miniature IBM cells. And we who lived amongst these dehumanized men know what humanity looks like when you take away the individual . . .

We reject this concept of humanity. We believe in a humanity made of individuals and not robots. That is why we chose to fight for the truth and the integrity of each and every human being.

Censorship is the central fact of the writer's life in every authoritarian society. In some states the regime creates or controls organizations of writers so as to ensure that no word put down on paper can be a threat to that regime's comfort and security. In the U.S.S.R., the Writers Union serves that function. One of its members, the highly popular author Georgy N. Vladimov, resigned in 1977 because the Writers Union had kept from him an invitation from his Norwegian publisher to go to the Frankfurt Book Fair to publicize his novel *The Faithful Russian*. The novel was published abroad in 1975, but in Vladimov's own country was circulated only in samizdat, the underground literature. It had been banned by the censors because it is a chilling tale of the Soviet prison camps. Although Vladimov had never served time in a camp, his mother, a professor of literature, had been sentenced in 1952 to ten years in a prison camp. Because of her imprisonment, Vladimov was not allowed to practice the law he was trained for. He made his living for a few years as a hauler, a ditchdigger, and a locksmith before discovering his calling as a writer.

Vladimov's first major book, *The Great One*, a best seller when it appeared in 1961, was translated into many languages. His second novel, *Three Minutes of Silence*, was held up by the censors for seven years before it was finally published. Resigning from the Writers Union meant breaking with the "official" world and depriving himself of a living as a writer. (After his resignation Vladimov became chairman of the unofficial Moscow chapter of Amnesty International.)

In an open letter to the Writers Union, Vladimov explained his withdrawal:

> All attempts to control literature will be as inevitably unsuccessful as projects for perpetual motion machines. Literature cannot be controlled. It is, however, possible either to help or to hinder a writer in his extremely difficult task. Our mighty Writers Union has invariably preferred to do the second, since it has always been, and continues to be, an apparatus of the police . . .
>
> Persecuting and expelling everything rebellious, questioning, or "incorrect," everything that was the strength and flower of our literature, you have destroyed the source of any genuine personality in your own Union. While this source remains—whether

in a man or in an association—there is still hope of change, repentance, rebirth. But now . . . we have reached the point of no return: the fate of writers whose books are bought and read is in the hands of writers whose books are not bought or read . . .

I continue to live in this country but I wish to have nothing more to do with you. Speaking not only for myself but on behalf of all those you have expelled, all those you have "marked" for destruction and oblivion—they have not authorized me to do this but I do not think they will object—I exclude you from my life . . .

Bear the burden of being grey, do what you are suited for and what you are called to do—oppress, persecute and confine. But count me out. I am returning card no. 1471.

Whatever Vladimov writes now may appear in French, English, German—but never in his native language, in his own country. If some of his books are published in Russian, it will be in the West; the term for that is *tamizdat* (literally, "published over there," meaning books published in Russian, but abroad).

One of the most jealously protected state secrets in countries of the Soviet bloc is the book which lays down policy for the censors. Recently the book of secret instructions prepared by the Polish bureau of censorship was smuggled out of the country and published in England. The Polish emigré writer Jan Kott, reviewing the book for the American press, said:

> *The Black Book of Polish Censorship* for the first time shows censorship in totalitarian countries as a complete system for the transformation of reality into "unreality" . . . Facts do not exist

for the censorship's semantic system until published . . . One's own industry never pollutes rivers in a socialist country. The reality accepted by the censors allows only a neighboring country's industry to pollute rivers. Of course with the exception of Russia . . . Censorship as a system does not aim at protecting the socialist state against open criticism (about this one even fears to think!). As a semantic system it protects and secures from criticism not the state and the system, but rather their ideal models. Censorship is the creation of an ideal image of the state and the nation. In this ideal model of a state there is no room, for instance, for alcoholism (Poland is one of the most alcoholic countries in the world) . . . In the ideal state plagues do not kill cattle and insects do not destroy crops . . . Even accidents never happen . . .

As for the fate of the writer under such censorship:

A Censorship order can condemn a writer to total nonexistence by a prohibition against both publishing his work and mentioning his name in print.

The size of a book's printing and permission to reprint are also controlled by censorship in spite of a book's popularity, and even more so when it is popular.

Freedom of speech and press are solemnly proclaimed in the Constitution of the Polish People's Republic. In Poland there is no "censorship," because the word "censorship" is censored by censorship. Censorship does not even call itself censorship. Only the Bureau exists.

In Czechoslovakia, censorship is as severe as anywhere in the Communist regimes of Eastern Europe. In the Prague "Spring" of 1968, writers showed themselves to be the most powerful force for liberalization. That literary freedom ended with the

Soviet invasion of Czechoslovakia. The American dramatist Arthur Miller, past president of International PEN, has pointed out the paradoxes of the writers in Czechoslovakia:

> Almost alone among writers deprived of liberty, the Czechs did once possess it. It is many centuries now that a literate class of people flourished in that country, and if it was not independent politically for most of its history it was at times the most productive center of culture in Europe. In recent years, of course, the levels of freedom in Czechoslovakia were no different than anywhere else in the West, and its people long ago identified themselves as democratic in the ordinary Western usage of that concept.
>
> Thus, I suppose it is the one case, at least in Europe if not world-wide, in which the freedoms of communication were taken from a people rather than not yet achieved. So that one cannot possibly adopt what might be called the anthropological attitude here—the viewpoint that these people, after all, had never known or particularly cared about the purely Western notions of individual freedom, and so their anguish at the absence of them is less theirs than their observers'. In the Czech case it is not a case of writers having failed to achieve freedom but of being stripped of the freedom they unquestionably possessed . . .

Czech writers, too, have resorted to circulating typed copies of their manuscripts among themselves and their friends. Since 1972 some 120 such typed volumes by more than fifty authors have appeared: they are called "Padlock Publications." They reached ever-widening circles as the quantity and quality of officially published works deteriorated. A recently issued list of books officially available included only four original literary works in Czech or Slovak; most of the other titles were translations. Writers who refuse to be shackled—and these include most of the new and most talented authors—are denied admittance to the Czech Writers Union. They therefore cannot be published officially, and the underground press is their only outlet.

Some Czech writers have been arrested and accused of "subversion of the Republic" for having sent banned manuscripts out of the country for publication. Nevertheless, one of them, the playwright Vaclav Havel, in a 1977 interview with the BBC filmed clandestinely in Czechoslovakia, showed hope for his country's future:

> It is up to everyone, all of us, to decide what our future will be like. You can't keep excusing everything by the omnipotence of the government and the helplessness of the citizen . . . People are . . . beginning to desire a freer, more dignified self-realization. Young people travel many miles to various semi-official concerts by nonconformist singers, people are copying new manuscripts of Czech authors, workers are no longer willing to sign just anything that is put before them. These things may seem to be marginal but I believe that this new awakening represents our main opportunity for the future.
>
> A free spirit and independence of thought by the individual is the source and recondition of a society's outward freedom. The more people are able to think and act as free human beings, in keeping with their human dignity and conscience, the more difficult it will be for the authorities to maintain the various repressive measures by whose means they keep their citizens in thrall. I am thus an optimist in the long term because I do believe that in history life in the end triumphs over the repressive pressures of a power apparatus.

Writers in East Germany have shown such an independent spirit that when their national literary congress met in 1978 the government forbade many of the most prominent authors to attend it. "Obviously the Communist Party does not dare start an open discussion at this time," said Stefan Heym, a novelist who was one of those excluded. He, like most of the others banned from the congress, had protested the exiling of Wolf Biermann, a dissident poet and singer, in 1976. Biermann, called the Pete Seeger of his country, was not permitted to return home after a singing tour of West Germany. Many of the works of East German authors have been published abroad but are denied print at home. As if to remind the Communist regime of unpleasant parallels, several exhibits of the works of German writers who went into exile during the Nazi era have recently toured Europe. The same thing is happening again as East German authors, whose manuscripts had to cross the border to get published, have followed their books into exile.

The Biermanns of the totalitarian societies have created the underground song, the most popular of all the varieties of unofficial culture. In the Soviet Union the best-known poet-singer was Alexander Galich, who after emigrating in 1974 died suddenly in Paris three years later. His witty, satirical songs and his lyric poems won him an international audience. With samizdat literature, such songs share the task of keeping alive the realities of Soviet life censored from the media. Tape recordings are used to disseminate underground songs, creating the process known as *magnitzdat* ("publishing by tape recorder"). Galich said that he chose the medium of the song because he knew thousands of people could carry it in their heads, thus ensuring that what he had to say would reach a large audience and be remembered.

The pioneer of this genre was Bulat Okudzhava, a lyric poet, and one of the giants in the field along with Galich. Of equal importance is Vladimir Vysotsky, described by a Russian artist as "the volcano of the modern Russian soul." Vysotsky's repertoire covers a great range, and much of it is presented in the official media. The songs he has written for magnitzdat, however, divide into three broad kinds, according to a British specialist in Russian studies, Gerry Smith. The first "present mercilessly realistic episodes from the everyday life of Soviet citizens and portray this life as brutish, untouched by official ideology, and relieved only by fierce forays into alcohol and sex. These songs are informed by a clear-eyed understanding of and compassion for ordinary people that is absolutely beyond the reach of officially approved writing: it is social realism of a high artistic order and shows up for what it is the crippling sham of the official dogma of Socialist Realism."

The second kind is songs of criminal- and labor-camp life. "Whereas the songs of everyday life challenge orthodoxy by proclaiming the irrelevance of the approved ideology for the life of ordinary people, the criminal songs present an alternative ideology. This ideology rests on a rejection of civilized conventions and a resorting to a fiercely competitive ethos of ruthless individualism . . ."

The third and extreme end of Vysotsky's repertoire is "a relatively small number of songs in which he speaks on his own account as a member of the Soviet cultural elite and tells of the personal and professional pressures that this status entails."

The story of Pa Chin, a Chinese novelist once nominated for the Nobel Prize, offers an example of the artists and writers who were purged during Mao's Cultural Revolution, which started in 1966. Not until 1978 was anything heard of most of them. After ten years of "purgatory," Pa Chin decided to break his silence through an interview at his home in Shanghai with two French journalists. From October 1966 to early 1970, Pa Chin was ordered to report daily to the Writers Association offices in Shanghai. Not for literary purposes, but to clean toilets, unblock drains, sweep floors, and wait on tables. On the main streets of Shanghai big posters appeared, calling him a "traitor to China."

Born in 1904, Pa Chin published his first novel at the age of twenty-five. His novels often deal with young people, for his special concern is with those reaching the age when they will shoulder the responsibility for their country. His chief characters in most of his novels are rebels and revolutionaries. His work was very popular with the educated young readers of China in the decades before the Communist victory of 1949. Although not a party member, he was entrusted with leading positions in publishing and the literary associations.

Yet it was thought necessary to "re-educate" him in 1966. Although never physically ill-treated, he said he was "morally brutalized." He was forced into "self-criticism"—confessing sins and errors, real or not—at sessions attended by large crowds and broadcast on television. His political rights were taken away, as well as his right to write. His two children were sent away, forced to do heavy labor in the country. The decade was a tragic waste of time; what he regretted most was not being allowed to write.

In 1972, after Mao Tse-tung and Chou En-Lai intervened, he was rescued from a "re-education" center and allowed to translate Russian books. But he was still not permitted to do his own writing and was kept under constant surveillance. Not until May 1977 was the last ban lifted. He told the journalists he felt "confident about the future of Chinese literature and art, now that the policy of 'letting a hundred flowers bloom' has been revived." As for his own writing, he is working on a book "describing the life of writers who, like myself, suffered for ten years. I want to accuse and express my indignation."

9

An American
Commitment . . . Abroad

Human rights—the ways in which governments treat their citizens—became a central theme in American foreign policy in 1977. When President Carter gave his Inaugural Address, he said, "Because we are free we can never be indifferent to the fate of freedom elsewhere . . . Our commitment to human rights must be absolute." The President had entered the White House protesting against the "cynical, manipulative" methods of the Nixon-Kissinger era. After Vietnam and Watergate many Americans felt there was no moral underpinning to our government. In foreign policy, previous administrations had appeared to be ready to accommodate to any regimes willing to serve our strategic interests, regardless of their human rights practices. But in his government, Carter declared, *people* would come first.

The taking of a moral position on international affairs is, of course, not new. To some, the Carter voice sounds like an echo of Woodrow Wilson's. Nongovernmental organizations in the United States had long ago placed human rights on their agenda, and Congress had been making moves on the issue for several years. But the White House had refused action until President Carter joined with Congress and put the Executive Office at the service of human rights. With the adoption of the UN covenants and the Helsinki pact, human rights everywhere became not only the business of other states but their obligation to protect.

Of all the issues the Carter Administration has espoused, the human rights policy is the most popular. "It seems," said Vice President Mondale, "that this country needs a mission: not in a messianic way, but if we're going to feel good about our society we have to project our most attractive values— freedom, justice, an open society . . ."

Easy to declare, such a human rights policy has been much harder to carry out. For human rights as an aim of foreign policy can run headlong into other aims, sometimes with higher priorities. How do you balance those conflicting aims? This has proved to be the most complicated of foreign policy questions. The rights themselves are already defined in various basic documents. The problem is how to determine what constitutes violations of human rights. And if you can do that, what steps can an administration take either to press for the observance of human rights or to retaliate for their violation?

After defining America's concept of human rights in a speech made at the University of Georgia Law School early in 1977, Secretary of State Cyrus Vance raised questions about how to apply it: "In pursuing a human rights policy, we must always keep in mind the limits of our power and of our wisdom. A sure formula for defeat of our goals would be a rigid, hubristic attempt to impose our values on others . . . We must be realistic. Our country can only achieve our objectives if we shape what we do to the case at hand."

He was saying that in the case of each country we need to know the kind, the extent, the trend of violations of human rights. Would our action improve matters or make them worse? Would taking measures—cutting off food supplies, financial aid—against a government that violated human rights penalize the poor and hungry who have no responsibility for what their government does? Should we negotiate quietly to rectify injustices, or should we blast violators of human rights in the press and public forums? There is no formula, he concluded, which can provide automatic answers to such questions.

It sounds like an argument for flexibility, a term that upsets many who recall how flexibly morality was bent under previous administrations. But neither would rigidity serve a foreign policy that must be realistic if it is to have any chance of being effective. What goals are practical over what period of time? And what means does government have to achieve its purposes? The United States has many means: economic and technical aid, food, military weapons and alliances, its influence in international-aid agencies. Which means do you use in specific circumstances? Always bear in mind that conditions change, and you need to estimate what pressures under the changing conditions of a given country have a chance to bring about the desired result. Because situations around the world vary so much, the application of any human rights policy will give the impression of inconsistency.

Then, too, how much right do we have to intervene in the affairs of another country? Of course our foreign policy, like that of other countries, is directed in theory to advancing or protecting the interests of our own state. The problem is how to determine what those interests are. To the average reader of the press our human rights policy seems to be inconsistent. People ask why the United States pressures one country for its violation of human rights but not another. Why Brazil and not Korea? Why Argentina and not the Philippines? The answer has to do with determining what the American interests are in each case and then weighing those which may be in conflict.

If you keep in mind the myriad of social, racial, ethnic, political, religious groups within the United States, you will perceive how hard it is to establish a consensus on policy. Polish Americans, for instance, are intensely concerned about United States policy on Poland, blacks about policy on Africa, Jews and Moslems on the Middle East. American banks make loans to foreign countries and businesses; our corporations build plants abroad or buy into foreign companies. An assured supply of oil is important to an America short of energy; there are dozens of minerals and other products found only abroad which are essential to our economy. We have military bases in foreign countries, alliances with various nations and blocs of nations . . . The list of interests—economic, political, strategic—is long, and often, when human rights concerns collide with other interests, they may take a back seat.

Critics of United States policy on human rights approach the issue from different perspectives. There are some, like Senator Daniel P. Moynihan, who wish to see human rights used as a political tool of American foreign policy, not simply as a humanitarian program. The Senator believes that "the central political struggle of our time is that between liberal democracy and totalitarian communism." He then applies that conviction to the handling of foreign policy:

It is entirely correct to say that quiet diplomacy is effective in obtaining concessions from totalitarian regimes with respect to particular individuals who seek our help. But the result of proceeding in this fashion is that the democracies accommodate the dictators. (The dictators let the occasional prisoner out of jail in return for our silence about those jails.) Concepts of human rights should be as integral to U.S. foreign policy as Marxism-Leninism is to Soviet operations and planning.

If the Foreign Service prevails, we will soothe the Soviet Union. But the Soviets are necessarily singled out by any serious human rights offensive—and they know it. They are the most powerful opponents of liberty on earth today. Their ideology remains, since the eclipse of fascism, as the only major political doctrine that challenges human rights in principle . . .

From the left comes a different criticism of American policy on human rights. Two professors, Noam Chomsky of the Massachusetts Institute of Technology and Edward S. Herman of the University of Pennsylvania, call for just as aggressive a policy as Senator Moynihan, but one directed at another set of states. To them United States pursuit of democracy abroad is as much a myth as was our benevolent involvement in Vietnam:

This myth has remained unruffled even in the face of the accelerating Brazilianization of the Third World over the past decade, very often under active U.S. sponsorship, with frequent displacement of democratic governments and extensive and growing resort to repression, including physical torture, imprisonment, death squads, and mysterious "disappearances," all within the U.S. sphere of influence. In this context the state which has sponsored and supported the Somoza family [Nicaragua], the Shah [Iran], Marcos [the Philippines], Park [South

Korea], Pinochet [Chile], Suharto [Indonesia], and the Brazilian generals can announce a campaign for human rights throughout the world and be taken with the utmost seriousness.

The authors present a table of ten countries* in Latin America and the Third World which have been mainly within the United States orbit since World War II. It aims to show graphically how American-controlled aid has been positively related to possibilities of profitable investment climate and inversely related to the maintenance of a democratic order and human rights. The conclusion reached is that

the pattern revealed is clear, persistent, rational, and ugly. Human rights have tended to stand in the way of the satisfactory pursuit of U.S. economic interests—and they have, accordingly, been brushed aside, systematically. U.S. economic interests in the Third World have dictated a policy of containing revolution, preserving an open door for U.S. investment, and assuring favorable conditions of investment. Reformist efforts to improve the lot of the poor and oppressed, including the encouragement of independent trade unions, are not conducive to a favorable climate of investment . . . There is also a convergence of economic and military-strategic interests in support of Third World fascism, as the military juntas in charge usually have a client relationship to the U.S. military establishment, are cooperative on U.S. bases, and specialize in the cleaning up of any subversives and protestors who challenge the satellite relationship.

The view of Chomsky and Herman is that since World War II the "Washington connection" has been strongly correlated

---

* *Brazil, Chile, Dominican Republic, Guatemala, Indonesia, Iran, Philippines, South Korea, Thailand, Uruguay.*

with the proliferation of regimes of terror and oppression, because that is what has made for a "more favorable investment climate." Investment criteria come before considerations of human rights. Under "conservative" administrations the United States aggressively supports the authoritarian regimes of client states; under "liberal" administrations, the United States provides support, but seeks at the same time at least some concessions on human rights. The result at bottom is the same, they believe.

A quick review of the problems of economic and military aid to other countries helps put the issue into perspective. Such aid is usually of two kinds: bilateral, in which the United States provides help by itself, and multinational, in which international financial institutions (there are half a dozen) supported by many nations offer loans to applicants. When it came into office, the Carter Administration formed an interagency committee to work out a policy on how to apply human rights criteria to the various forms of foreign aid. Congress had already taken a hand here; back in 1974 it had begun to order cuts in military assistance to such nations as South Korea, Chile, and Uruguay on human rights grounds. Generally it barred military and economic aid to countries which consistently violated human rights. And to police that decision, it ordered the State Department to file an annual report on the human rights practices of each country that might get military aid. Another step it took was to provide that Congress, by joint resolution, could cut off military aid or arms sales to any government consistently and grossly violating human rights. The Carter Administration, early in 1977, cut military aid to Argentina, Uruguay, and Ethiopia, and published a critique of human rights practices in countries receiving aid. Taking offense at this criticism, Argentina, Brazil, El Salvador, Guatemala, and Uruguay rejected military loans they had coming to them.

A careful watch has been kept on American foreign policy by national peace, religious, and social-action organizations. (Typical ones are described in Chapter 11.) Acting like a coordinated Helsinki Watch Group, a coalition of forty such organizations issues periodic reports on the government's economic and military aid program. It welcomed meetings between United States officials and democratic opposition leaders of other countries, and the stepping up of efforts to obtain freedom for prisoners of conscience, as well as the occasional withdrawal of support from repressive regimes by the international financial institutions in which the United States has a vote.

But the coalition observed that after more than a year in office the Carter Administration was continuing to spend millions of American tax dollars to support governments guilty of severe human rights violations. It protested especially the high levels of military aid given to four governments—Nicaragua, the Philippines, Indonesia, and Iran—whose records in human rights were among the worst.

South Korea and the Philippines are examples of repressive governments that count almost entirely on the United States for their survival. American pressure on them could be decisive. Yet President Carter gives them continued support, citing strategic and national security interests as overriding considerations.

To illustrate how much the United States aids dictatorships which grossly violate human rights, the coalition published a chart for the fiscal year 1977:

U.S. AID TO DICTATORSHIPS, FISCAL YEAR 1977
(in millions of $)

	ECONOMIC AID	MILITARY AID	U.S. FINANCIAL INSTITU-TIONS[1]	U.S. FUNDS THROUGH INTER-NATIONAL BANKS[2]	TOTAL
South Korea	81.7	293.7	349.9	143.6	868.9
Philippines	84.0	68.1	76.2	142.7	371.0
Indonesia	140.9	57.6	80.2	131.2	409.9
Thailand	17.2	95.4	17.1	66.5	196.2
Chile	43.8	—	16.9	51.6	112.3
Argentina	—	36.8	72.7	244.8	354.3
Uruguay	0.2	—	3.6	19.6	23.4
Haiti	11.1	—	—	8.9	20.0
Brazil	4.6	60.2	118.5	351.3	534.6
Nicaragua	22.9	3.3	17.8	36.7	80.7
South Africa	—	—	57.9	83.2	141.1
Total	406.4	617.7	810.8	1280.1	3115.0

[1] Export-Import Bank. Commodity Credit Corporation export sales, Housing Investment Guarantees. [2] World Bank, Asian Development Bank, Inter-American Development Bank, International Monetary Fund. Note: Includes 1976 transition quarter (July-September 1976). Prepared by the Center for International Policy, 1977.

Aid to such countries is supposed to cement a friendly relationship with the government in power, which will be of strategic importance to America. But, says the coalition, "in such cases no argument is made that either the present government is challenged by an external power or that any changes in government would be inimical to U.S. interests. The unstated implication seems to be that by giving or selling arms, the U.S. will have greater influence with the present government. But what real substantial national security objectives will be achieved by granting security assistance are not stated. This is most probably because the State Department has none that will withstand public and congressional scrutiny. In the meantime, the U.S., through such aid relationships, commits itself in fact to supporting suppression of opposition to the recipient government—the very opposite of a real human rights policy."

Take Iran, in revolution as this book was being completed. It is an example of the controversy over United States aid to violators of human rights. "In the past 30 years the U.S. has sold more than $18 billion worth of arms to Iran and has helped organize and equip a vast security system that gives its ruler, Shah Mohammed Riza Pahlevi, absolute control of the country," said *The New York Times* not long before the crisis erupted. What was the United States giving the Shah and what did the critics say about it? Iran bought $5.8 billion in arms in fiscal year 1977, $3.0 billion in 1978, and was eligible for a proposed $2.6 billion in 1979. Highly sophisticated equipment was on the list: fighter planes, guided missiles, destroyers. It also included small arms and training for the SAVAK (secret police) and Iranian Army units involved in repressing internal opposition to the Shah's rule.

But, reported Amnesty International, Iran had "the highest rate of death penalties in the world, no valid system of civilian courts and a history of torture which is beyond belief." The Shah's notorious reputation for disregarding human rights seemingly would have called for ending or reducing such massive arms sales, especially that equipment designed for use in internal repression. The Carter Administration admitted that Iran's arms requirements "exceed those strictly necessary for making its borders unattractive to aggression or for maintaining internal stability." Yet the administration justified such arms sales as essential to "the maintenance of peace in the Persian Gulf, by fostering in Iran a sense of confidence in its security." Ironic, coming just before that confidence was destroyed by mass upheaval.

The coalition interpreted these facts as proof that the Carter Administration "intended to continue the effort to build Iran into a minor superpower—a process begun when the Shah was brought to power in a CIA-sponsored coup in 1954. The result of the massive arms sales to Iran, however, has been greater regional *instability* with neighboring states (Iraq, Saudi Arabia and Kuwait), hastening to match Iran's purchases both quantitatively and qualitatively with their own buildups. More than that, the continuing sales of advanced weapons systems which require the presence of huge numbers of American technicians (up to 50,000 by the 1980s, according to the Senate Foreign Relations Committee), more deeply implicate the U.S. in support of one of the world's most repressive and militaristic regimes."

What did the Shah give in exchange for American support? He pledged to protect the vital routes out of the Persian Gulf that carry over half the oil used by the West. More—the profit of American business from his purchases of arms and technology was enormous. In 1977, for instance, the United States took in about $6 billion from Iran and paid out $3.5 billion, mostly for oil. That was almost $2 coming in for every $1 going out. Yet this was all placed in great danger by the totally unforeseen popular rebellion against the Shah's rule.

South Africa's apartheid policy has become a major focus of popular protest in recent years. The fact that it is the only country in the world which by law denies human rights to its citizens purely on the basis of race is an outrage to simple dignity and decency. The continuing investment of private citizens, banks, and corporations in South Africa raises an issue of morality versus profit. As evidence of the Carter Administration's declared stand for human rights, the Department of Commerce banned American sales to the South African military and police forces. But some government actions support apartheid. The United States finances trade with South Africa through the Export-Import Bank. It allows American companies credit on their income tax for taxes paid to the South African government. Here, too, as with Iran and many other nations, trade and military considerations affect foreign policy.

President Carter believes greater American business involvement in South Africa will lead to changes in apartheid. (He saw that happen to race relations in the South during the civil rights struggle of the 1960s.) If enlightened business insists on modification of the system of separating whites and blacks by law, then the injustice of the police state should gradually be eased. And eventually true freedom, equality, and democracy will prevail. That idea was behind the program started by the Reverend Leon H. Sullivan of Philadelphia. More than one hundred U.S. corporations subscribed to it. The "statement of principle" they signed calls for them to work for non-segregation of the races and for equal-employment practices in their South African plants, to bar job fragmentation and restriction on apprenticeships for blacks, and to recognize the freedom of black workers to form or join unions. To determine what progress is being made, the companies are asked to make periodic reports.

The United States is South Africa's largest trading partner, its second-largest overseas investor, and the supplier of nearly one-third of its overseas credit. American credits and investments total close to $5 billion. More than four hundred U.S. corporations operate there, including many of the largest. The reason is the high rate of profit—made possible by super-exploitation of the blacks. American companies receive returns on their investments of between 17 and 25 percent annually.

Apart from the obvious motive of self-interest, American business claims its investments in South Africa provide jobs and hence a better standard of living for their black employees. South African officials echo the claim, warning that a pull-out of American business would cause the greatest suffering to the very people—the blacks—it is intended to benefit, depriving them of jobs and any hope of entering the middle class. Most American corporations investing in South Africa oppose withdrawal and divestiture. Their investments open up economic opportunity, which is the way to end apartheid, they say.

But a lengthy documented report on United States corporate interests in South Africa (prepared by the subcommittee on African affairs of the Senate Foreign Relations Committee and the Congressional Research Service) concluded that American corporate interests have *strengthened* the economic and military status quo in South Africa. The effect has been to undermine American foreign policy, which aims at "a progressive transformation of South African society toward free political participation." Citing the report's findings, many began calling for active discouragement of American investment in South Africa.

American students have been among the most vocal advocates of ending the alliance between American business and

South Africa. They have demanded that their universities sell their stocks in South Africa and withdraw their deposits from banks that lend to the government of South Africa. The University of Massachusetts at Amherst sold its stocks in companies with holdings in South Africa. Other schools said they would dispose of such stocks in companies that did not support the so-called Sullivan principles. Several American trade unions pledged to withdraw deposits from banks continuing to make loans to the South African government. The National Association for the Advancement of Colored People, in 1978, called for full economic sanctions against South Africa to bring about a showdown. This was a shift from its earlier policy, shared with the National Urban League, of trying to change the apartheid policy through pressure from American investors. The NAACP became convinced that only complete withdrawal and divestiture has a chance to work.

If the voice of South Africa's blacks could be heard, it is likely that the majority would oppose foreign investment in their country. According to the Christian Institute of South Africa, an organization of church people opposed to apartheid, "Blacks accept that the consequent economic recession and unemployment would cause them suffering, but argue that this would be for a limited period by contrast with the unending suffering caused by the continuation of apartheid."

With the Soviet Union and its Communist satellites in Eastern Europe the United States does not have the capacity to alter conditions to the degree to which it could with South Korea, the Philippines, Iran, and South Africa. The history of American relations with the Communist regimes has been erratic. In the days of the Eisenhower Administration there was much propaganda about the "liberation" of Eastern Europe from Soviet control. But when Russia crushed rebellions in Hungary and Czechoslovakia, the United States offered only rhetorical aid to the dissidents. When Nixon and Kissinger pursued a policy of détente, it appeared to some that America had tacitly given up trying to improve the plight of people living under Communism's rigid control. A new situation emerged, however, with the signing of the Helsinki Agreement in 1975. As we have seen, the commitment of the United States, the U.S.S.R., and thirty-one other nations to human rights encouraged dissidents in the totalitarian nations to hope for internal reforms. They have tried to bring about democratic change through their own efforts combined with outside pressure.

What has been the result of the human rights policy as directed toward the Soviet Union? The Kremlin's great displeasure over the raising of the issue could be expected in a country where the violation of human rights is built into the authoritarian system. The Russians have proved resistant to external pressure for change. And Soviet dissidents have paid high penalties for publicly voicing their demand for a more human society. Could the United States do more than it has to advance the cause of human rights in the U.S.S.R.? The attempt to get the Soviets to ease Jewish emigration by offering trade concessions did not work. President Carter's pressure in the Shcharansky, Ginzburg, and Orlov cases only resulted in heavier sentences at the end of trials that were a farce by Western legal standards.

Some Americans have urged all along that the human rights policy carries the risk of endangering détente—peaceful coexistence with the Soviet Union—and that nothing is worth the risk of a nuclear war between the two great powers. Such critics assume that stressing human rights somehow makes nuclear conflict more likely. But the Russians have repeatedly said that ideological warfare with the West will continue, regardless of détente. If the Soviet press can attack the political and social system of the West, why cannot the West criticize their system?

Perhaps one barrier to understanding the issue is disagreement over what détente means. When the Russians use the word, they focus it narrowly on the questions of arms control and trade. Like us, they see nuclear disarmament as a matter of life and death. They want to limit an arms race for economic reasons, too. Less investment in the military means more resources available to meet human needs. And we both think increased trade between us would be beneficial. So each side sees the SALT negotiations—a strategic arms treaty—as the centerpiece of détente.

Beyond that, however, each side's struggle for worldwide strengthening of its power and influence inevitably inflames suspicion and rouses old hostilities. When to the clashing of interests in such places as Africa and the Middle East you add the issue of human rights and political freedom, the discord grows. The Soviets seem to believe that human rights is an "artificial" issue. Internal political control is crucial to Communist authorities: it is hard to believe they will ever permit free speech at home just to please public opinion abroad. One U.S. State Department advisor on Soviet policy, Professor Marshall D. Shulman, has cautioned that "easing repression [in the U.S.S.R.] is more likely to result from evolutionary forces within the society under prolonged conditions of reduced international tension than from external demands for change and the siege mentality they would reinforce."

Is there, then, an irreconcilable conflict between seeking détente and supporting human rights? Two moral obligations are involved. The United States, as one of the great nuclear powers, has the duty to try to reduce the danger of nuclear war by negotiations with the Soviet power. Obviously this is a priority for all governments as well as our own. We also are pledged to press for human rights everywhere in the world including the U.S.S.R. Are we guilty of cynical and callous indifference to the fate of Soviet citizens if we do not insist upon Soviet observance of human rights as a prior condition to détente?

Since we know what is at stake for humanity in the nuclear arms race, it seems elementary wisdom to place regulation of military competition first. For if détente is not achieved, there will be no chance to work for strengthening of democratic values anywhere. Peace, too, is a human right.

To accept that position does not mean one condones violations of human rights by the Soviet Union, or by any other regime or society. After developing this approach to the issue, Professor Shulman suggests we view human rights in this light:

The ultimate interest of democratic societies does require that they work for an international environment in which democratic values can survive and flourish by a constant projection and encouragement of democratic norms of behavior. What can and should be projected, however, are not particular institutions, such as the capitalist system or the two-party system, which, in any case, individual nations will adopt according to their own preferences; rather, what is essential to promote are those common ethical values such as the commitment to justice, liberty, equality, human dignity and to civil and tolerant discourse, reflecting the emphasis in democratic values on the process rather than on the realization of particular ends. What this implies is that the effort to enlarge the international sense of community be bound not to a particular form of world order but to a process of peaceful change toward the fuller realization of these values.

10

...and at Home

How safe are the human rights of the American citizen?

If you ever wrote a critical letter to the White House, marched in an antiwar demonstration, or joined a civil rights group, your name may be in the files of the police, the FBI, or the CIA.

For more than fifty years members of the American Friends Service Committee (AFSC) were the victims of government surveillance. Their telephones were tapped, their mail opened, and their actions spied upon without court warrants. The AFSC got access to the files kept upon it through the amended Freedom of Information Act of 1975. At least ten government agencies, including the FBI, the CIA, the Secret Service, and the various armed forces, had the AFSC on their "watch list." Why? Because the Friends openly supported school integration and the civil rights struggle? Because they openly opposed military preparedness, the war in Vietnam, and the growth in power of the military-industrial complex?

The maintenance of such intelligence files stifles dissent by making citizens fearful of exercising their First Amendment rights. ("Congress shall make no law . . . abridging the freedom of Speech or of the Press; or the right of the people peacefully to assemble and to petition the Government for a redress of grievances.") You may think twice about speaking out or joining up if you suspect your name will appear in an intelligence file. For political radicals and trade unionists to be spied upon, harassed, and blacklisted is an old story. But recent decades have seen social activists of all kinds—people organizing to eliminate poverty, inequality, and injustice—subject to surveillance.

In Chicago, an FBI police raid killed two Black Panther leaders, Fred Hampton and Mark Clark. Groups in Puerto Rico and New York advocating Puerto Rican independence were for eleven years the target of an FBI campaign of disruption. For thirty-eight years the FBI spied upon the Socialist Workers Party, using a total of sixteen hundred informers. It burglarized the SWP's office in New York ninety-two times. The offices and files of various peace groups in the late 1960s and early 1970s were often bugged, burglarized, vandalized, and burned, yet police could find no suspects.

Local and state police have an even worse record than the FBI and CIA in violating the First and Fourth Amendments. (Article IV: "The right of the people to be secure in their persons, houses, papers, and effects, against unreasonable searches and seizures, shall not be violated.") The names of millions of "agitators" were placed in local police intelligence files, files full of hearsay and personal information, often sexual, laying their subjects open to blackmail, harassment, or worse. While public disclosure laws have affected the CIA and FBI, local police can still operate in almost total secrecy.

One estimate holds that the security bureaucracy in the United States was spending $7 billion per year at one time, imitating authoritarian regimes. In extensive hearings before the U.S. Congress, ample evidence was produced to show that the spying agencies not only kept track of their victims but resorted to "dirty tricks"—forgeries, provocations, and raids. Abroad, official agencies of the American government attempted assassinations of foreign leaders. "The CIA's recent record," wrote John Stockwell, one of that agency's former officers, "includes the assassinations of Patrice Lumumba; Ngo Dinh Diem, the South Vietnamese President; Rafael Trujillo Molina, the Dominican Republic President; Gen. René Schneider, the commander in chief of the Chilean Army; plus several bloody covert wars, and a deadly terrorist program in Vietnam called Phoenix that the CIA says involved the killing of 22,000 Vietnamese."

Another facet of CIA activity violating human rights has received relatively little attention. This is its corruption of the communications media abroad by buying up publications, press services, radio and TV stations, and using them to transmit false news and propaganda. The practice had a dual effect: it not only subjected people abroad to lies on a massive scale, but the false news was picked up innocently by reporters for American media and then disseminated here at home. If democracy is to survive, it requires an informed people. The wealth available to the CIA enabled it to corrupt the foreign press for subversive purposes. Such was the actual process in the CIA's overthrow of the Guatemalan government in 1954, and it was part of the CIA's operation in Chile in 1973.

Yet government officials who want to clean their hands by

disclosing the illegal practices they were party to or aware of are silenced. Public disclosure of snooping against political critics and the press embarrasses government leaders. "The watchword of every administration," said Representative Elizabeth Holtzman, "seems to be: silence the whistle blowers. Ergo the case of Frank W. Snepp, 3d, the former CIA agent against whom the Government won a civil suit charging that he violated a secrecy agreement when he published a book, *Decent Interval*, about his experiences with the agency. Censoring Mr. Snepp, who is appealing the decision, would impose a silence on hundreds of recently fired CIA operatives who otherwise might expose ugly secrets."

No recent administration, she went on, has taken the First Amendment seriously enough to prosecute its violators fully. Plea bargaining has been permitted top officials, while the lower level has been excused on the ground that they were merely carrying out orders. Her fellow members in Congress, she pointed out, have not done much better: "Restrictions on demonstrations near embassies, the failure to enact a newsman's privilege law, and the reluctance to impose stricter controls on the FBI and the CIA all underline the unwillingness of Congress to protect First Amendment rights aggressively."

In a public declaration at the time of the 1977 Belgrade meeting on implementation of the human rights provisions of the Helsinki accord, a large number of American activists challenged the claim of the Carter Administration as well as the other governments at Belgrade that they were defenders of human rights.

The American cases they listed began with the Wilmington Ten, black activists who contended they were political prisoners railroaded into jail in North Carolina for their civil rights advocacy. The three people who testified against them during the trial have now admitted they told lies under police pressure. Responding to national and international pressure to exonerate the prisoners, the state's governor cut their sentences by about one-third, but refused to pardon them.

Others cited in the statement as victims of persecution were Puerto Rican nationalists, American Indian activists, and "the thousands of anti-war activists, Black freedom fighters, feminists, socialists and others who fight for social change . . . The government's own documents have proven its systematic efforts to disrupt, destroy and introduce violence into movements for civil rights and social change in the U.S."

Then, taking up the deprivation of social and economic rights, the signers of the statement presented the grievances of large blocs of people:

- Thousands of foreign-born workers, driven to seek jobs in the United States illegally because U.S. corporations perpetuate poverty in these workers' home countries, live in subhuman conditions in the United States, subject to deportation by the U.S. government if they dare to stand up for their human and democratic rights . . .
- There are 40 million poor Black, Hispanic, American Indian, and Asian-American people . . . They are without employment opportunities, decent housing, or proper medical care, and have no way of emerging from poverty. They are suffering still more as the government continues to attack their hard-won rights to affirmative action in employment, education, and housing . . .
- Women, struggling to defend their reproductive freedom . . . to win ratification of the Equal Rights amendment, and to win funding for expansion of child-care facilities . . .

• And millions of workers, peasants, and intellectuals around the world [who] know the truth about the priority of human rights in United States foreign policy because they live under brutally repressive regimes the United States government props up in Iran, Chile, Brazil, South Korea, Argentina, South Africa, the Philippines, Indonesia, and elsewhere.

The signers went on "to denounce the violations of the principles of socialist democracy in the Soviet Union and Eastern Europe," listing many examples country by country.

Amnesty International, which views human rights from a narrower perspective, listed eighteen "prisoners of conscience" in its 1977 report on the United States (among them the Wilmington Ten). Andrew Young, the chief U.S. representative to the UN, once compared dissidents in the Soviet Union to civil rights campaigners in the United States. He said, "In our prisons too there are hundreds, perhaps even thousands, of people whom I would call political prisoners" and added that he himself had been a political prisoner when arrested in a civil rights demonstration in Atlanta ten years before. Immediately criticized for his statement, Young denied he had meant to equate the status of political freedom in America with that in the Soviet Union. "I know of no instance in the U.S. where persons have received penalties for monitoring our Government's position on civil or human rights," he said.

As one reader of *The New York Times* put it, "Mr. Young confuses the mistakes and injustices that inevitably occur under any system with imperfections of the system itself. They are not flaws of the system, but human failings independent of ideology. What we don't have in America is the total harnessing of society's institutions and powers to a predetermined political end. We don't have the concerted subversion of the judicial process as a means of social control. Even in his lame attempts to back off from his first pronouncements Mr. Young cannot see the difference between less than perfect implementation of a noble policy and the deliberate enforcement of an ignoble one . . ."

For black Americans like Andrew Young, the phrase "noble policy" may stick in the throat. Blacks cannot erase the memory of enslavement for two hundred years under the American democracy, and the discrimination and segregation which have been its aftermath. Nor can Native Americans forget that white settlers on their land sought to and almost succeeded in extinguishing the people they found here. The rights nobly proclaimed by the Founding Fathers have never been equally available to all Americans, especially those of color.

To the left of Ambassador Young there is the radical view of America as "one vast jail with invisible walls. Those who are actually behind bars are not criminals, but political prisoners whose misdemeanors amount to nothing compared to the felonies of the elite." The system of private property is blamed for dispossessing and dehumanizing the poor and the black.

While so extreme a position may be held by few, the government itself acknowledges how far it has yet to go to fulfill the promise of social and economic rights for all. In a report issued in 1978, the U.S. Commission on Civil Rights said that little progress has been made toward the nation's goal of social and economic equality for women and members of ethnic minorities. Women and male members of minorities significantly trailed nonminority men in the fields of education, employment, income, and housing. Government statistics for the 1960–76 period showed some improvement for women and minorities, but there was "clear documentation of many continuing and serious problems of inequality."

Human rights as they apply to women in the United States have been the subject of both federal and state laws. Women gained the important political right of the franchise long ago. But the first civil rights legislation to deal with discrimination against working women did not come until the Equal Pay Act of 1963. This act calls for equal pay for equal work, but it is full of technical loopholes and is unevenly enforced. The 1964 Civil Rights Act was the most comprehensive bill to outlaw sex discrimination. Several Executive Orders since then have enlarged the rights of women, and in 1967 an Age Discrimination Act applied to women as well as to men. Many states have fair-employment laws, but most do not forbid discrimination based on sex. The New York State Human Rights Law, to take one example, outlaws sex discrimination, but although it is one of the best state laws, its enforcement and implementation have been lackadaisical, at best. Women have come to feel it is a waste of time to file complaints with the State Division of Human Rights which administers the law. To go into court for action requires money few complainants—women or minorities—can afford.

It is at a time of crisis that human rights are most commonly in danger. In most societies, such rights are often sacrificed to what is perceived to be the desperate need to survive. That perception, of course, may be mistaken or, what is worse, faked to give those in power the excuse to trample on their citizenry. The Nixon Administration's constant invocation of "national security" as justification for its flagrant violation of constitutional rights is but one example. "Security" has cloaked many a nefarious White House operation almost from the beginning of our democracy. The internment of 110,000 Japanese Americans in World War II was explained away on the ground of military danger. And the threat of Communism was used to sweep aside the Bill of Rights after both world wars. When a crisis is invoked to dispense with human rights, one must always be on guard. It is hard to conceive any crisis which could justify taking away those few minimal rights the philosopher Charles Frankel has termed universal (see p. 13). Is torture required to develop a country? Are concentration camps necessary for economic and social development? Does putting a gag on every citizen's mouth advance the public welfare? What kind of emergency calls for the suspension of rights for years, decades, generations?

On balance, how good or bad is the American record on human rights? Taking the long view, Professor Frankel believes we have been "much too defensive" about the American system of government:

> For all that may be wrong with that system it is deeply inscribed in our Constitution that people are entitled to privacy, that they are entitled to be treated with dignity and with respect for their physical security, that they have a right to due process with respect to the police, and to freedom of worship. These are guarantees that we should be proud of. To those who say they are just a façade, or expressions of bourgeois prejudice, we should reply, I think, "So much the better for the bourgeois, let's all be bourgeois in these respects at least." For all of our lapses, I think that it's rare in human history to have a system of government that perseveres over any length of time in respect to such rights, and that has empowered citizens to defend those

rights regardless of the government's convenience. What we have in our country is a difficult kind of achievement, unusual in the record of human experience. It shows lack of perspective and of elementary self-respect to be silent or apologetic with regard to it, and not to say, when challenged, that it is a system of rights that is good for us, and that we think it is also good for others.

11

Who Is Doing What?

If there is one thing that is clear from this discussion, it is that there is no easy way to guarantee human rights. How do we achieve equity and justice in human society? How do we secure all persons and peoples freedom and dignity? In a Declaration of INTERdependence he drafted in 1975, historian Henry Steele Commager pointed out the ways:

> We hold these truths to be self-evident: that all men are created equal; that the inequalities and injustices which afflict so much of the human race are the product of history and society, not God or nature; that people everywhere are entitled to the blessings of life and liberty, peace and security and the realization of their full potential; that they have an inescapable moral obligation to preserve those rights for posterity; and that to achieve these ends all the peoples and nations of the globe should acknowledge their interdependence and join together to

dedicate their minds and their hearts to the solution of those problems which threaten their survival.

Many have accepted the moral obligation to struggle for human rights. By the 1970s almost everything that could be done to write human rights into law had been accomplished. Covenants, protocols, and legislation exist. But laws are not self-executing. Almost every state in the world at some time, or all the time, ignores the rights it proclaims. For that reason human rights organizations have been created in every part of the world. In structure they are basically of two kinds: governmental organizations (GOs) and non-governmental organizations (NGOs). Their function is to provide information and organize action. (Some consider their primary aim the former, intending that what they communicate will lead others to action.)

Without knowledge of violations of human rights there could be no action, of course. The sources of information are many, though never sufficient, for those who violate rights are not likely to broadcast their crimes. Information can be gathered from government reports and from the reports of NGOs. Individual petitions for help contain facts or allegations, and then there are hearings conducted by both public and private groups. Finally, press reports convey information gathered in the field.

What courses of action are possible when violations have been determined? There are several available to both GOs and NGOs. States or international bodies can legislate to make illegal certain kinds of violations. Both GOs and NGOs can investigate charges to obtain full disclosure of the facts. They can provide help to victims. They can adjudicate claims. They can negotiate with governments in the hope of improving policy and practice. Where resistance to change is encountered they can publicize the violations to create pressure for change from within and without. They can educate the public to a greater awareness of human rights and to create the determination to protect them. And finally, a step rarely taken, governments, lone or in concert, can use physical force or other coercive measures, such as economic pressure, against offending governments.

The United Nations, with its covenants, protocols, and commissions, is the first agency one thinks of when considering how best to protect human rights. But as of this writing, less than one-third of the world's governments had ratified the UN Covenants on Human Rights. (Although President Carter signed the covenants on behalf of the United States in 1977, they must be ratified by the Senate before they take effect. It is not known when he will submit them for ratification.) Decades after the adoption of the UN Universal Declaration, the president of the International League for Human Rights (NGO) could make this somber judgment of the record of its Commission on Human Rights:

> At the U.N., the Commission on Human Rights has shown an inability to deal effectively, indeed, deal at all with human rights violations. Egregious complaints from individuals and groups have been ignored for political reasons. No effective action has been taken on such vital matters as religious intolerance, the repression of freedom of expression, freedom of movement, the rights of non-citizens, abuse of the administration of justice. Non-governmental organizations are frustrated and

even harassed in their efforts to redress these violations before the UN.

Disillusionment with the UN stems from the failure of its Human Rights Commission to make use of its powers to deal with a single case of gross violations. The only cases to be treated thus far by the UN have been charges against South Africa, Chile, and Israel, and none of these came through the commission's channels. When NGOs bring up violations before UN bodies, diplomatic protocol protects nations by an unwritten rule against "naming names" and supplying concrete facts about victims and violators. Offended by the few occasions when NGOs spoke up boldly to the powers of the world, the UN took retaliatory action designed to suppress public complaints on pain of suspension of the NGO's consultative status. It also moved the Human Rights Commission from New York to Geneva, thus isolating human rights from the international nerve center. Disillusionment was deepened when, in 1975, a General Assembly resolution equated Zionism with racism, attributing to Zionists a belief in the racial inferiority of the Arab peoples. To many NGOs it seemed the ultimate step in playing politics with human rights. A study of UN actions shows "selective morality" or a double standard at work: violations of human rights are criticized only in some parts of the world when such violations are virtually worldwide.

Is the UN's existence, then, worth nothing in regard to human rights? At the least, it has set standards. Taken together, the various international agreements give us a worldwide code of human rights morality and law. The UN's educational programs have helped awaken the world's conscience. And many of the UN's specialized agencies—those dealing with problems of health, food, labor, education, children, refugees—make important contributions to human rights in their own way.

The big failure is in providing the necessary means for dealing with violations of human rights in particular countries. Implementation measures, where they exist at all, have not gone much beyond paper commitments. Can the UN's member states ever be expected to rise above their selfish ideological or political interests and form their judgments on the standard of simple justice?

Sometimes there seems to be movement in the right direction. In 1978, for the first time, the Human Rights Commission named Uganda and Cambodia as violators against which it had taken confidential measures. In the past, Third World bloc voting had saved these highly publicized violators from UN scrutiny. But now some Third World powers joined Western rights advocates in placing Uganda and Cambodia on the same list as Indonesia, Equatorial Guinea, Ethiopia, Bolivia, South Korea, Malawi, Uruguay, and Paraguay.

At the same time, however, efforts to get the commission to draft a convention against torture failed, nor was there any advance on the proposal to establish a UN High Commissioner for Human Rights. And the traditional targets—Chile, Israel, and South Africa—continued to get the brunt of the criticism.

An alarming turn for human rights took place, almost unnoticed, at the UN General Assembly in 1977. The Assembly decided that individual rights were no longer a principal concern. Two new priorities stressing collective and national rights were adopted. The new first priority is to combat violations of

the "human rights of peoples"—with apartheid, racial discrimination, and colonialism leading the list of violations, and
aggression and threats against national sovereignty, national
unity, and territorial integrity included. Protests that the vital
rights of the individual would be subordinated to those collective rights were voted down.

The second new priority was "the realization of the New
International Economic Order . . . [as] an essential element
for the effective promotion of human rights and fundamental
freedoms." Again there were protests that this is not necessarily
true, that abundant experience drawn from both developing
and developed countries shows higher economic standards are
not inevitably linked to improved human rights. Indeed, one
student of developing nations, Harold R. Isaacs, has observed,
"Never have more 'liberated' people become more subject to
more tyrannies in the name of achieving more freedom . . ."

Writing in *The Washington Post*, William Korey said that
"the New International Economic Order, however useful its
purpose, has little, if anything, to do with human rights. It
represents the aspiration of developing countries to restructure
the world economy for their own benefit. The focus is upon
benefits to be derived by Third World states, not necessarily
their populations. Given the structures of most Third World
countries, it is an open question whether economic benefits
have raised the standard of living of more than their elites."
In the voting on the new priorities, almost three-quarters of
the support came from authoritarian regimes of the right
or left.

There are other international and regional governmental
agencies concerned with human rights, but they, too, like the
UN's Human Rights Commission, provide more rhetoric than

action. They tend to play a passive role because they can move only to the extent their state members permit. And these are guided by narrow national interest. *Realpolitik* dictates a double standard. Decisions about whether or not to take action are made not on general ethical standards but by political and economic calculation. When one reads statements issued on human rights, it is useful to measure them against these realities. Equatorial Guinea, for example, will condemn the Ian Smith regime for denying Rhodesian Africans their civil and political rights, while the dictatorial Equatorial Guinea government denies its own people civil and political rights.

Apart from the numerous governmental organizations, there are a host of private, voluntary groups committed to the protection of human rights. They function in almost every country, although far more are found in the West. There are many kinds; perhaps one way to classify them is by their relation to government. While remaining private, some are created on the initiative of government, or at least encouraged to form by the tax-exempt status offered them. Others, banned by government, exist as secret, illegal groups. In some places, such as the Soviet Union, NGOs like the Helsinki Watch Group are seemingly tolerated because the government signed the Helsinki Pact. But their small and exposed membership, as we have seen, has been picked off one by one and sent to prison or labor camps on manufactured charges of illegal conduct.

Another way to look at the NGOs is from the perspective of their special interest in human rights. Some limit themselves to a single aspect (dissenters in mental hospitals, labor, Moslems, lawyers, journalists), some to violations in one country (Iran, Indonesia, Chile), or to a region of the world (South Africa or East Europe), or to one class of violation (torture). Through the natural way people form groups around common interests, it is likely that most kinds of human rights violations get some attention. Political tradition and cultural bias inevitably affect choice of issues. Which explains why the Western groups generally pay more attention to civil and political violations than to economic and social violations.

For many years after the UN placed human rights on its agenda the issue was ignored or neglected. The best-known activist group, Amnesty International, in London, was not founded until 1961. Here in the United States the first group was organized in New York in 1966. The number of members remained relatively small until AI won the Nobel Peace Prize in 1977. With the consequent flood of publicity on its aims and methods, AI expanded rapidly. By June 1978 it had 200,000 individual members and supporters in 107 countries, an increase of 103,000 members and supporters and 29 countries over 1975–76. The concern generated for human rights was also reflected in the large number of conferences on the issue, in the variety of professional associations offering panels on human rights at their meetings, in the proliferation of research projects, articles in scholarly and popular periodicals, and in the expansion of school and college courses on human rights. (Lagging behind, however, was funding for human rights research.)

To describe all the human rights groups in the United States alone would take far too many pages. This book contains a resource list (see page 157) which names some of the major ones and will guide the reader to more than five hundred other groups and publications dedicated to human rights. So multifarious has the field become that a communications network was recently established by university professors to facilitate exchange and interaction among activists, academics, and governmental and intergovernmental officials working on human rights. (Called Human Rights Internet, it publishes an invaluable *Newsletter* nine times a year from its offices at 1502 Ogden St., N.W., Washington, D.C. 20010. Some of its issues run to over fifty closely packed pages.)

Amnesty International is a permanent organization with an exclusive focus on human rights. Its concern is the plight of the world's prisoners of conscience. Independent of any government, political faction, ideology, or religious creed, AI believes "every person has the right to hold and express his convictions and he has an obligation to extend the same freedom to others." It works for the release of men and women imprisoned anywhere for their beliefs, color, language, ethnic origin, or religion, provided they have not used or advocated violence. This is what AI means by "prisoners of conscience." AI also opposes the use of torture and the death penalty in all cases without reservation. It advocates fair and early trials for all political prisoners and works on behalf of persons detained without charge or trial, and those detained after sentence has expired.

AI estimates that there are at least a quarter of a million people in jail today principally for their beliefs. (There are certainly many more than that, but precisely how many is not known, since governments do not release figures.) To persuade governments to set such prisoners free, or at least ameliorate their conditions, is AI's task. At its international headquarters in London, a staff of a hundred researchers with regional responsibilities follows news of arrests, investigates cases of prisoners, and monitors governmental repression. Their main sources of information are press and broadcast reports, letters from strangers, and their own global membership. When the facts meet AI's investigatory standards, a case sheet is made up for the adoptable prisoner, and that person's case is then assigned to working groups of AI members of a different nationality from the prisoner. The adoption group bombards the government and prison officials in question with letters urging reconsideration of the case and release of the prisoner. It also writes embassies, leading newspapers, international organizations, organizations related to the prisoner's occupation, and the prisoner's relatives and friends. When possible, its members provide financial aid to the prisoner's family. In critical situations AI may send distinguished jurists or diplomats to attend controversial trials or plead for the life of a sentenced victim.

AI members from various occupations and professions write letters, send appeals, or take other measures to intercede for their imprisoned colleagues in other countries. Prisoners in extreme danger may be helped by AI's Urgent Action Network. Members who write letters for months or years in behalf of an adopted prisoner begin to feel a close kinship with the prisoner. (Sometimes, when their campaign is successful, they may meet the person they've helped free.) An intensive run of patient, pleading letters and the publicity they engender has succeeded in wearing down even the most hardened government.

Governments have the power of amnesty, and what AI does is to bring the prisoner's file again and again and again to the jailer's attention. By constant nagging it has made governments listen. Not all of them, of course. But its gadfly methods have worked well enough to help secure the release of more than 13,000 prisoners in the first sixteen years of its existence. To what degree it was AI's pressure that brought results is not easy to determine. AI has no political power based on strategic control of wealth or armed force, nor does it even have the strength of sheer numbers. It must rely on a shared belief in the morality of its cause and the credibility of its information. It may shame some governments into action, but mostly it works by damaging their reputation in the eyes of influential others—their own people, their political and military allies, their trading partners, international investing agencies, and the like.

To further its goal, AI sends international missions to investigate conditions in specific countries. Reports of findings are printed and publicized. AI issues a monthly *Newsletter* on its work throughout the world, an Annual Report, and a regular series of Briefing Papers—human rights reference booklets on individual countries. One of its regular publications is *A Chronicle of Current Events*, a journal of the human rights movement in the Soviet Union which provides in English translation the samizdat texts written by Soviet citizens. AI also exerts influence through its consultative status or cooperative relationship with the UN and several of its divisions, as well as with other international groups.

The International League for Human Rights (ILHR) is another of the more prominent nongovernmental organizations. The oldest of the groups devoted to the protection of international human rights, it was founded in France in 1902, as a response to the Dreyfus case, and called the International League for the Rights of Man. A few years ago it changed its name to the present one. Headquartered in New York, it has made the UN the principal arena for its work. It has been a prime mover in shaping international law to human rights. Nonpartisan, it draws its funds entirely from voluntary contributions. Unlike other NGOs, it is a confederation of many national civil liberties organizations working principally to further human rights in their own countries, though some direct their attention abroad, too. Most of the affiliates are North American or Western European. The others are thinly scattered in Latin America, Africa, the Middle East, and Asia. There is only one affiliate in the Communist world—the Moscow Human Rights Committee (founded in 1970), which has been grimly persecuted by the Soviet government. Understandably, then, the league has a Western-liberal bias, for few NGO groups can be found in either Third World or Communist nations—unless they exist as opposition groups in exile.

The ILHR's growing disillusionment with the UN's role in human rights has already been mentioned. Recently the league helped form a Lawyer's Committee on International Human Rights, in response to complaints of alleged violations of human rights, which reach the league's office at a rate of a thousand per year. The lawyers are experimenting with efforts to intervene through "class action" methods. The league sends observers to political trials, dispatches special missions to conduct on-site investigations of human rights, and prepares reports for congressional committees and the public. By such means it tries to shape public opinion in accordance with its convictions. Over the years it has been a catalyst of other human rights groups and a bridge between them.

Study of the league's Annual Review shows actions of many kinds taken in connection with human rights violations in dozens of countries around the world, ranging from detailed accounts of conditions found by the missions to Paraguay to a 300-page report documenting the consistent pattern of violations in the Republic of Guinea. Through protests, petitions, letters, delegations, news releases, the league resists moves toward repression and strives to create a better climate for human rights.

Beyond the human rights groups set up exclusively for that purpose are many organizations which have established standing committees to patrol this front. To cite but two examples: the Committee on Scientific Freedom and Responsibility (CSFR) and the International Freedom to Publish Committee (IFPC). The former was set up by the American Association for the Advancement of Science (AAAS) in 1976. In its first year it created a clearinghouse on persecuted foreign scientists, reviewed individual claims of violations of scientific freedom in the United States, and studied alternative due process and appeal mechanisms for scientists and engineers who are harassed and punished by employers for blowing the whistle on wrongs committed where they work. The project grew so rapidly the AAAS soon hired a Human Rights Coordinator. CSFR runs workshops on human rights and scientific freedom, issues background papers on persecution of scientists in individual countries, and coordinates the visits to the United States of foreign scientists who have been victims of persecution by their governments. It also arranges for testimony before international and regional human rights commissions and has sent the AAAS president abroad to voice the concern of the American scientific community over violations of human rights in the countries visited.

The International Freedom to Publish Committee was

created by the Association of American Publishers in 1975. Active in it are many of the executives of leading American publishing houses. It selects a small number of needy writers or publishers in various parts of the world and tries to help them survive the repressive conditions under which they live and work. It has helped writers obtain visas to go abroad, where they can report on conditions in their country, it has gained the release of several from prison, it has protested to many governments the harassment of their writers, it has publicized cases of censorship and literary repression. Members have testified before Congress and addressed symposia on aspects of publishing and human rights. IFPC has joined with the American PEN and AI on various campaigns. The committee's actions are both public and private, ranging from open publicity in the press to quiet attempts to influence American and foreign government policy.

Most of the human rights organizations, whether national or international, are Western in origin. Their leadership comes from the middle class, much of it professionals and intellectuals. The groups do not have mass memberships nor are they committed to revolutionary change as a means of achieving justice in repressive societies. How much good can such groups do? Professor Laurie S. Wiseberg, a student of human rights, discusses that issue:

> It can be argued, quite convincingly, that all that the human rights NGOs have been able to accomplish with respect to Chile has been to save a few lives, to save a few people from torture, and to make prison life more bearable by Red Cross care-packages. One cannot, of course, quantify the value of a

human life or the suffering that a man endures; and this is not intended to demean those efforts.

On the other hand, we are left with a set of very brutal statistics: roughly 20,000 killed or "disappeared" and one million out of a population of ten million driven into exile. One can, therefore, legitimately ask whether human rights NGOs do not, in some ways, simply mop up the psychological consequences of repression—i.e., make it easier for the affluent in affluent nations of the world to live with their consciences because they have committed some time and some money to the cause of human rights.

Whether to support human rights organizations or to support revolutionary movements that offer some hope of greater change is a personal decision that arises in part from one's assessment of the feasibility of revolutionary success and from one's assessment of the probability of actualizing justice through the revolutionary process . . . Yet it can be argued that human rights organizations, even if they are not prepared to join the revolutionary struggle by taking up arms, provide psychological support to indigenous forces who must—in the end—bear the burden of overthrowing the tyrannies which oppress them . . .

Wiseberg then cites the question Ginetta Sagan of Amnesty International has been studying: Could the gas chambers of the Hitler Reich have existed if there had been an organization like Amnesty International active at that time? Sagan is investigating the 1933–39 period in Nazi Germany. Her premise is that Hitler's internment of all dissenters was not unlike the present situation in many countries. Hitler's prewar victims were the equivalent of today's prisoners of conscience. If an organization like AI had been functioning in the 1930s, with a worldwide network of volunteers reporting on such violations of human rights, would not the crimes of Nazism have been exposed to the world's view? Could Hitler have been stopped? Could the Holocaust and World War II have been averted?

12

What You Can Do

"But what can I do?"

A question we inevitably ask ourselves after reading the long catalogue of deprivation, humiliation, terror, and death.

A former prisoner of conscience in Turkey, the lawyer Mumtaz Soysal, had this to say:

> Human rights will not be protected if left solely to the governments of this world. Individuals of good will must everywhere concern themselves with and act to curb repression, and to defend human rights. *The ordinary individual can make a difference.* This is the experience of Amnesty International. An aroused public opinion is a powerful weapon. Important as bills of rights and legal mechanisms are, still more important is the concern of one individual for another, one group for another, one nation for another. The active concern of public opinion is everywhere of help. But nowhere is it more essential than when an individual human being remains helpless before a

repressive regime, a cowed national community, and an inadequate international machinery for redress.

"The ordinary individual can make a difference . . ." Rights are effective only if we stand up for them. Human values will survive only if we resist oppression. We cannot stand silent while we wait for a more humane world order. If we act, we often have no way of knowing if our action brought about results. Still, we must act to show our belief in standards of decency no government can violate with impunity, our faith in our ability to protect human rights even in the face of today's realities.

"Rights are the one feature that distinguish law from ordered brutality," says legal philosopher Ronald Dworkin. "If the government does not take rights seriously, then it does not take the law seriously either." Governments that do not take the law seriously may include our own, at times, or they may be far away. But each of us can reach out and touch the lives of the victims of such lawlessness. Their fate, and the fate of thousands of others, depends upon our ability to make their plight known. The everyday welfare of many millions in countries whose oppressive systems are bolstered by our country's actions depends in part upon our ability to reshape our government's policy.

What then can you do, if you are concerned about human rights?

As an individual you can join any one of the human rights organizations. Amnesty International, for instance, through which you can enter or form a small group, adopt a prisoner of conscience, and work for his or her release. Or the many other organizations whose names and addresses can be found through use of the Bibliography. Write for their literature and choose which you want to support.

You can look around your own community to see what violations of human rights are occurring, and how they are either being redressed or ignored. Join or form a local group concerned about protecting those rights.

News of human rights abroad appears regularly in the newspapers and periodicals you read. You can study the issues, and make yourself a resource person for information leading to action in your community, student, or professional organization.

There are many nongovernmental organizations whose primary concern may not be human rights. In most of their programs, however, there are points of principle which can be linked to human rights. You can ask your school, church, temple, civil or professional organization to take up those human rights issues that most immediately touch them.

The more people who develop an interest in them, the greater the chance of improving the condition of human rights. Help inform the public by asking your libraries (school, public, organizational) to buy and feature books and films on human rights and to display human rights materials.

The public officials who represent us on every level—local, state, and national—need to know their constituents are concerned about human rights. As private citizen or as member of an organization you can call to the attention of your U.S. Representative or Senator the current status of United States ratification of international covenants and conventions affecting human rights. Ask for their position on them. You can keep posted through the press on the administration's policies affecting human rights and decide which deserve your support and which your criticism. Let the White House know your position. And not only on foreign policy. Vigilance on domestic violations of human rights is just as important. Local officials—the police, the mayor, the city council—can be monitored to get them to live up to the rights pledged our own citizens.

Whatever we do, it is well to remember that there is no easy solution to the problems of inequity and injustice in human society. "We live in a world," writes Ludwig Raiser, a scholar of constitutional law, "a world echoing in all directions with reports of poverty, hunger, and misery, of exploitation and oppression of great masses of people, of the arrests, tortures, and assassinations of innocent victims by politically radical revolutionary groups or by greedy robbers, of the suppression of any freedom of expression by dictatorial regimes, including the freedom to confess one's own religious belief—of any number of incidents, in other words, which reveal a frighteningly widespread disdain for and degradation of human personhood."

In such a world, people of conscience cannot turn their backs upon the fate of humanity.

BIBLIOGRAPHY

The literature on human rights is large and rapidly increasing. A short book of this kind cannot pretend to cover it all. Happily, the need for specialized resource and bibliographic directories has been recognized and I refer the interested reader to them.

Human Rights Internet Newsletter, 1502 Ogden St., N.W., Washington, D.C. 20010. Published nine times a year, it reports on activities of human rights organizations of all kinds (in the United States and abroad), on books, articles, monographs, meetings, seminars, and other events. Internet's membership includes the key leadership of human rights groups internationally, and a core of scholars working in this field. It is not politically partisan and has no program of activism apart from its function as a communications network. $15/year.

Human Rights Organizations and Periodicals Directory, issued biennially by the Meiklejohn Civil Liberties Institute, Box 673, Berkeley, Calif. 94701. An alphabetical guide to organizations and agencies (nearly 500 entries) and the periodicals issued by them, plus a subject index. Most of the groups listed are national in scope; some are international. $3.

Human Rights Action Guide. Issued annually by the Coalition for a New Foreign and Military Policy, 120 Maryland Ave., N.E., Washington, D.C. 20002. It includes the addresses of organizations working on domestic aspects of human rights as well as those concentrating on foreign countries, and recommends books, pamphlets, audio-visual materials. 10 cents.

Information may also be obtained from the major nongovernmental human rights organizations. I list only some of the more active ones.

American Friends Service Committee, 1501 Cherry Street, Philadelphia, Pa. 19102. Issues reports, organizing materials; supplies books, films, slide shows through its Human Rights Program.

Amnesty International, 2112 Broadway, New York, N.Y. 10023. The U.S. headquarters of the worldwide human rights organization. It publishes annual reports on human rights conditions, special reports on various countries and on such issues as torture, and issues both a monthly *Newsletter* and the quarterly *Matchbox.*

Center for International Policy, 120 Maryland Avenue, N.E., Washington, D.C. 20002. A research group which publishes reports analyzing U.S. foreign policy on human rights as it affects various parts of the world.

Clergy and Laity Concerned (Human Rights Coordinating Center), 1114 G Street, S.E., Washington, D.C. 20003. It monitors human rights legislation, offers literature, films, speakers, and publishes regularly a compilation of news articles and resources on human rights.

Helsinki Watch Committee, 205 East 42 Street, New York, N.Y. 10017. It monitors violations in the U.S. and abroad of the human rights provisions of the Helsinki accords, documenting and publicizing them.

In addition, the following groups can be contacted for publications and newsletters to keep current on human rights needs and issues. Some of these, as well as those listed above, may have local groups working in your area.

Alternatives, 1924 East 3 Street, Bloomington, Ind. 47401.

Bread for the World, 207 East 16 Street, New York, N.Y. 10003.

Center of Concern, 3700 13 Street, N.E., Washington, D.C. 20017.

Interfaith Center for Corporate Responsibility, 475 Riverside Drive, New York, N.Y. 10027.

Office of International Justice and Peace, United States Catholic Conference, 1312 Massachusetts Avenue, N.W., Washington, D.C. 20005.

United Nations Association of the U.S.A., 300 East 42 Street, New York, N.Y. 10017.

P E R I O D I C A L S

These publications regularly provide information on human rights:

A Chronicle of Current Events, Journal of the Human Rights Movement in the U.S.S.R., Amnesty International, 2112 Broadway, New York, N.Y. 10023.
Columbia Human Rights Review, Columbia Law School, 116 Street and Amsterdam Avenue, New York, N.Y. 10027.
Human Rights Journal, Institute of Human Rights, 6 Place de Bordeaux, 6700 Strasbourg, France.
Index on Censorship, Writers and Scholars International Ltd, London. Distributed in U.S. by Random House, 201 East 50 Street, New York, N.Y. 10022.
Review, International Commission of Jurists, 109 Route de Chene, 1224 Chene Bougerie, Geneva, Switzerland.

B O O K S

The sources listed below are a selection of the books and articles I referred to in my research. I also made extensive use of current newspapers and periodicals, especially *Index on Censorship* and *A Chronicle of Current Events.*

Amnesty International. *Report on Torture.* Farrar, Straus & Giroux, 1975.
Arendt, Hannah. *The Origins of Totalitarianism.* Meridian, 1958.
Baraheni, Reza. *The Crowned Cannibals.* Vintage, 1977.

Bloch, Sidney and Peter Reddaway. *Psychiatric Terror: How Soviet Psychiatry Is Used to Suppress Dissent.* Basic Books, 1977.

Brownlie, Ian, ed. *Basic Documents on Human Rights.* Clarendon Press, Oxford, 1971.

Carey, John. *UN Protection of Civil and Political Rights.* Syracuse University Press, 1970.

Chomsky, Noam and Edward Herman. *The Political Economy of Human Rights.* 2 vols. South End Press, 1979.

Chomsky, Noam and Edward S. Herman. "The US versus Human Rights in the Third World." *Monthly Review,* v. 29, no. 3 (July–August 1977), pp. 22–25.

Cranston, Maurice. *What Are Human Rights?* Taplinger, 1973.

Da Fonseca, Glenda, ed. *How to File Complaints of Human Rights Violations: A Practical Guide to Inter-Governmental Procedures.* World Council of Churches, Geneva, 1975.

Deming, Richard. *Man and the World: International Law at Work.* Hawthorn, 1974.

Dworkin, Ronald. *Taking Rights Seriously.* Harvard, 1977.

Fried, Charles. *Right and Wrong.* Harvard, 1978.

Garling, Marguerite. *The Human Rights Handbook.* Facts on File, 1979.

Goulet, Denis. "Thinking about Human Rights," *Christianity and Crisis* (May 16, 1977).

Henkin, Louis. *The Rights of Man Today.* Westview, 1978.

Klare, Michael and Nancy Stein. "Exporting the Tools of Repression," *Nation* (October 16, 1976).

Kyemba, Henry. *A State of Blood.* Ace, 1977.

Larsen, Egon. *A Flame in Barbed Wire: The Story of Amnesty International.* Norton, 1979.

Miller, Allen O., ed. *A Christian Declaration on Human Rights.* Eerdmans, 1977.

Nielsen, Nils C., Jr. *The Crisis of Human Rights.* Nelson, 1978.

Nielson, Winthrop and Frances. *The UN: The World's Last Chance for Peace.* Mentor, 1975.

Osadchy, Mykhaylo. *Cataract.* Harcourt, Brace, Jovanovich, 1976.

Owen, David. *Human Rights.* Norton, 1978.

Petras, James. "President Carter and the New Morality," *Monthly Review*, v. 29, no. 2 (June 1977), pp. 42–52.

Polis, Adamantia and Peter Schwab, eds. *Human Rights: Cultural and Ideological Perspectives*. Praeger, 1979.

Robertson, A. H. *Human Rights in the World*. Humanities Press, 1972.

Said, Abdul Aziz. *Human Rights and World Order*. Praeger, 1978.

Saunders, George, ed. *Samizdat: Voices of the Soviet Opposition*. Monad, 1974.

Sobel, Lester A. *Political Prisoners: A World Report*. Facts on File, 1979.

Sohn, Louis and Thomas Buergenthal. *International Protection of Human Rights*. Bobbs-Merrill, 1973.

Spinrad, William. *Civil Liberties*. Quadrangle, 1970.

Tuttle, James C., ed. *International Human Rights Law and Practice: The Roles of the United Nations, the Private Sector, the Government, and Their Lawyers*. American Bar Association, 1978.

Wiseberg, Laurie S. "Human Rights, International Relations Theory and Regime Change," presented at International Studies Association, Washington, D.C., February 22–25, 1978.

Wiseberg, Laurie S. and Harry M. Scobie. "The International League for Human Rights: The Strategy of a Human Rights NGO," *Georgia Journal of International and Comparative Law*, vol. 7:289 (1977), pp. 289–313.

Woite, Robert, ed. *International Human Rights Kit*. A World without War Publication, 1977.

Zavala, Silvio. *The Defense of Human Rights in Latin America*. UNESCO, 1964.

Following are reports of some symposia on human rights:

"Human Rights and United States Foreign Policy: A Symposium," *Virginia Journal of International Law*, vol. 14 (Summer 1974), pp. 591–701.

"Human Rights: A Symposium," *Texas International Law Journal*, vol. 12 (Spring–Summer 1977), pp. 129–330.

"Human Rights and Foreign Policy," *Georgia Journal of International and Comparative Law*, vol. 7 (Summer 1977).

Human Rights: A Symposium. The Columbia University Committee on General Education (Fall 1977).

Some pamphlets or booklets dealing with human rights:

Basic Needs and Human Rights, by Patricia Weiss Fagen, January 1978. Center for International Policy (address above). $1.

Human Ethics for a Sustainable Society: Linking Human Rights and Basic Needs, by Peter Henriot, October 1977. Center of Concern (address above). $.75.

Human Rights and Vital Needs, by Peter Weiss, September 1977. Institute for Policy Studies, 1901 Q Street, N.W., Washington, D.C. 20009. $.50.

The PQLI: Measuring Progress in Meeting Human Needs, by Morris D. Morris and Florizelle B. Liser. August 1977. Overseas Development Council, 1717 Massachusetts Avenue, N.W., Washington, D.C. 20036. $1.

Making Rights Matter: Economic Justice and Human Needs, by Alan Geyer. October 1976. Service Dept., United Methodist Board of Church and Society, 100 Maryland Avenue, N.E., Washington, D.C. 20002. $.25.

Human Rights: A Priority for Peace, ed. by James R. Jennings and Patricia L. Rengel, Fall 1975. Office of International Justice and Peace (address above). $.50.

Human Rights and the U.S. Foreign Assistance Program, Fiscal Year 1978. Part 1, Latin America; Part II, East Asia. 1977. Center for International Policy (address above). $2.50 each.

Human Rights, Human Needs: An Unfinished Agenda. January 1978. Office of International Justice and Peace (address above). $.75.

APPENDIX:
Selected Documents
on Human Rights

CHARTER OF THE
UNITED NATIONS
(Excerpts)

We the peoples of the United Nations determined

to save succeeding generations from the scourge of war, which twice in our lifetime has brought untold sorrow to mankind, and to reaffirm faith in fundamental human rights, in the dignity and worth of the human person, in the equal rights of men and women and of nations large and small, and
to establish conditions under which justice and respect for the obligations arising from treaties and other sources of international law can be maintained, and
to promote social progress and better standards of life in larger freedom.

and for these ends

to practice tolerance and live together in peace with one another as good neighbours, and
to unite our strength to maintain international peace and security, and
to ensure, by the acceptance of principles and the institution of methods, that armed force shall not be used, save in the common interest, and
to employ international machinery for the promotion of the economic and social advancement of all peoples,

have resolved to combine our efforts
to accomplish these aims

Accordingly, our respective Governments, through representatives assembled in the city of San Francisco, who have exhibited their full powers found to be in good and due form, have agreed to the present Charter of the United Nations and do hereby establish an international organization to be known as the United Nations.

ARTICLE 1

The Purposes of the United Nations are:

1. To maintain international peace and security, and to that end: to take effective collective measures for the prevention and removal of threats to the peace, and for the suppression of acts of aggression or other breaches of the peace, and to bring about by peaceful means, and in conformity with the principles of justice and international law, adjustment or settlement of international disputes or situations which might lead to a breach of the peace;

2. To develop friendly relations among nations based on respect for the principle of equal rights and self-determination of peoples, and to take other appropriate measures to strengthen universal peace;

3. To achieve international co-operation in solving international problems of an economic, social, cultural, or humanitarian character, and in promoting and encouraging respect for human rights and for fundamental freedoms for all without distinction as to race, sex, language, or religion; and

4. To be a centre for harmonizing the actions of nations in the attainment of these common ends.

ARTICLE 55

With a view to the creation of conditions of stability and well-being which are necessary for peaceful and friendly relations among nations based on respect for the principle of equal rights and self-determination of peoples, the United Nations shall promote:

(*a*) higher standards of living, full employment, and conditions of economic and social progress and development;

(*b*) solutions of international economic, social, health, and related problems; and international cultural and educational co-operation; and

(*c*) universal respect for, and observance of, human rights and fundamental freedoms for all without distinction as to race, sex, language, or religion.

ARTICLE 56

All Members pledge themselves to take joint and separate action in co-operation with the Organization for the achievement of the purposes set forth in Article 55.

CONVENTION ON THE PREVENTION AND PUNISHMENT OF THE CRIME OF GENOCIDE

Text of the Convention

The Contracting Parties,

Having considered the declaration made by the General Assembly of the United Nations in its resolution 96 (I) dated 11 December 1946 that genocide is a crime under international law, contrary to the spirit and aims of the United Nations and condemned by the civilized world;

Recognizing that at all periods of history genocide has inflicted great losses on humanity; and

Being convinced that, in order to liberate mankind from such an odious scourge, international co-operation is required:

Hereby agree as hereinafter provided:

ARTICLE 1

The Contracting Parties confirm that genocide, whether committed in time of peace or in time of war, is a crime under international law which they undertake to prevent and to punish.

ARTICLE 2

In the present Convention, genocide means any of the following acts committed with intent to destroy, in whole or in part, a national, ethnical, racial or religious group, as such:

(a) Killing members of the group;

(b) Causing serious bodily or mental harm to members of the group;

(c) Deliberately inflicting on the group conditions of life calculated to bring about its physical destruction in whole or in part;

(d) Imposing measures intended to prevent births within the group;

(e) Forcibly transferring children of the group to another group.

ARTICLE 3

The following acts shall be punishable:

(a) Genocide;

(b) Conspiracy to commit genocide;

(c) Direct and public incitement to commit genocide;

(d) Attempt to commit genocide;

(e) Complicity in genocide.

ARTICLE 4

Persons committing genocide or any of the other acts enumerated in Article III shall be punished, whether they are constitutionally responsible rulers, public officials or private individuals.

ARTICLE 5

The Contracting Parties undertake to enact, in accordance with their respective Constitutions, the necessary legislation to give effect to the provisions of the present Convention and, in particular, to provide effective penalties for persons guilty of genocide or of any of the other acts enumerated in Article III.

ARTICLE 6

Persons charged with genocide or any of the other acts enumerated in Article III shall be tried by a competent tribunal of the State in the territory of which the act was committed, or by such international penal tribunal as may have jurisdiction with respect to those Contracting Parties which shall have accepted its jurisdiction.

ARTICLE 7

Genocide and the other acts enumerated in Article III shall not be considered as political crimes for the purpose of extradition.

The Contracting Parties pledge themselves in such cases to grant extradition in accordance with their laws and treaties in force.

ARTICLE 8

Any Contracting Party may call upon the competent organs of the United Nations to take such action under the Charter of the United Nations as they consider appropriate for the prevention and suppression of acts of genocide or any of the other acts enumerated in Article III.

ARTICLE 9

Disputes between the Contracting Parties relating to the interpretation, application or fulfilment of the present Convention, including those relating to the responsibility of a State for genocide or for any of the other acts enumerated in Article III, shall be submitted to the International Court of Justice at the request of any of the parties to the dispute.

ARTICLE 10

The present Convention, of which the Chinese, English, French, Russian and Spanish texts are equally authentic, shall bear the date of 9 December 1948.

ARTICLE 11

The present Convention shall be open until 31 December 1949 for signature on behalf of any Member of the United Nations and of any non-member State to which an invitation to sign has been addressed by the General Assembly.

The present Convention shall be ratified, and the instruments of ratification shall be deposited with the Secretary-General of the United Nations.

After 1 January 1950 the present Convention may be acceded to on behalf of any Member of the United Nations and of any non-member State which has received an invitation as aforesaid.

Instruments of accession shall be deposited with the Secretary-General of the United Nations.

ARTICLE 12

Any Contracting Party may at any time, by notification addressed to the Secretary-General of the United Nations, extend the application

of the present Convention to all or any of the territories for the conduct
of whose foreign relations that Contracting Party is responsible.

ARTICLE 13

On the day when the first twenty instruments of ratification or accession have been deposited, the Secretary-General shall draw up a *procès-
verbal* and transmit a copy thereof to each Member of the United
Nations and to each of the non-member States contemplated in
Article 11.

The present Convention shall come into force on the ninetieth
day following the date of deposit of the twentieth instrument of ratification or accession.

Any ratification or accession effected subsequent to the latter date
shall become effective on the ninetieth day following the deposit of
the instrument of ratification or accession.

ARTICLE 14

The present Convention shall remain in effect for a period of ten
years as from the date of its coming into force.

It shall thereafter remain in force for successive periods of five
years for such Contracting Parties as have not denounced it at least
six months before the expiration of the current period.

Denunciation shall be effected by a written notification addressed
to the Secretary-General of the United Nations.

ARTICLE 15

If, as a result of denunciations, the number of Parties to the present
Convention should become less than sixteen, the Convention shall cease
to be in force as from the date on which the last of these denunciations shall become effective.

ARTICLE 16

A request for the revision of the present Convention may be made
at any time by any Contracting Party by means of a notification in
writing addressed to the Secretary-General.

The General Assembly shall decide upon the steps, if any, to be
taken in respect of such request.

ARTICLE 17

The Secretary-General of the United Nations shall notify all Members of the United Nations and the non-member States contemplated in Article 11 of the following:

(a) Signatures, ratifications and accessions received in accordance with Article 11;

(b) Notifications received in accordance with Article 12;

(c) The date upon which the present Convention comes into force in accordance with Article 13;

(d) Denunciations received in accordance with Article 14;

(e) The abrogation of the Convention in accordance with Article 15;

(f) Notifications received in accordance with Article 16.

ARTICLE 18

The original of the present Convention shall be deposited in the archives of the United Nations.

A certified copy of the Convention shall be transmitted to each Member of the United Nations and to each of the non-member States contemplated in Article 11.

ARTICLE 19

The present Convention shall be registered by the Secretary-General of the United Nations on the date of its coming into force.

UNIVERSAL DECLARATION OF HUMAN RIGHTS

PREAMBLE

Whereas recognition of the inherent dignity and of the equal and inalienable rights of all members of the human family is the foundation of freedom, justice and peace in the world,

Whereas disregard and contempt for human rights have resulted in barbarous acts which have outraged the conscience of mankind, and the advent of a world in which human beings shall enjoy freedom of speech and belief and freedom from any fear and want has been proclaimed as the highest aspiration of the common people,

Whereas it is essential, if man is not to be compelled to have recourse, as a last resort, to rebellion against tyranny and oppression, that human rights should be protected by the rule of law,

Whereas it is essential to promote the development of friendly relations between nations,

Whereas the peoples of the United Nations have in the Charter reaffirmed their faith in fundamental human rights, in the dignity and worth of the human person and in the equal rights of men and women and have determined to promote social progress and better standards of life in larger freedom,

Whereas Member States have pledged themselves to achieve, in co-operation with the United Nations, the promotion of universal respect for and observance of human rights and fundamental freedoms,

Whereas a common understanding of these rights and freedoms is of the greatest importance for the full realization of this pledge,

Now, Therefore,
The General Assembly

Proclaims this Universal Declaration of Human Rights as a common standard of achievement for all peoples and all nations, to the end that every individual and every organ of society, keeping this Declaration constantly in mind, shall strive by teaching and education to promote respect for these rights and freedoms and by progressive measures, national and international, to secure their universal and effective recognition and observance, both among the peoples of Member States themselves and among the peoples of territories under their jurisdiction.

ARTICLE 1

All human beings are born free and equal in dignity and rights. They are endowed with reason and conscience and should act towards one another in a spirit of brotherhood.

ARTICLE 2

Everyone is entitled to all the rights and freedoms set forth in this Declaration, without distinction of any kind, such as race, colour, sex, language, religion, political or other opinion, national or social origin, property, birth or other status.

Furthermore, no distinction shall be made on the basis of the political, jurisdictional or international status of the country or territory to which a person belongs, whether it be independent, trust, non-self-governing or under any other limitation of sovereignty.

ARTICLE 3

Everyone has the right to life, liberty and security of person.

ARTICLE 4

No one shall be held in slavery or servitude; slavery and the slave trade shall be prohibited in all their forms.

ARTICLE 5

No one shall be subjected to torture or to cruel, inhuman or degrading treatment or punishment.

ARTICLE 6

Everyone has the right to recognition everywhere as a person before the law.

ARTICLE 7

All are equal before the law and are entitled without any discrimination to equal protection of the law. All are entitled to equal protection against any discrimination in violation of this Declaration and against any incitement to such discrimination.

ARTICLE 8

Everyone has the right to an effective remedy by the competent national tribunals for acts violating the fundamental rights granted him by the constitution or by law.

ARTICLE 9

No one shall be subjected to arbitrary arrest, detention or exile.

ARTICLE 10

Everyone is entitled in full equality to a fair and public hearing by an independent and impartial tribunal, in the determination of his rights and obligations and of any criminal charge against him.

ARTICLE 11

(1) Everyone charged with a penal offence has the right to be presumed innocent until proved guilty according to law in a public trial at which he has had all the guarantees necessary for his defence.

(2) No one shall be held guilty of any penal offence on account of any act or omission which did not constitute a penal offence, under national or international law, at the time when it was committed. Nor shall a heavier penalty be imposed than the one that was applicable at the time the penal offence was committed.

ARTICLE 12

No one shall be subjected to arbitrary interference with his privacy, family, home or correspondence, nor to attacks upon his honour and reputation. Everyone has the right to the protection of the law against such interference or attacks.

ARTICLE 13

(1) Everyone has the right to freedom of movement and residence within the borders of each state.

(2) Everyone has the right to leave any country, including his own, and to return to his country.

ARTICLE 14

(1) Everyone has the right to seek and to enjoy in other countries asylum from persecution.

(2) This right may not be invoked in the case of prosecutions genuinely arising from non-political crimes or from acts contrary to the purposes and principles of the United Nations.

ARTICLE 15

(1) Everyone has the right to a nationality.

(2) No one shall be arbitrarily deprived of his nationality nor denied the right to change his nationality.

ARTICLE 16

(1) Men and women of full age, without any limitation due to race, nationality or religion, have the right to marry and to found a family. They are entitled to equal rights as to marriage, during marriage and at its dissolution.

(2) Marriage shall be entered into only with the free and full consent of the intending spouses.

(3) The family is the natural and fundamental group unit of society and is entitled to protection by society and the State.

ARTICLE 17

(1) Everyone has the right to own property alone as well as in association with others.

(2) No one shall be arbitrarily deprived of his property.

ARTICLE 18

Everyone has the right to freedom of thought, conscience and religion; this right includes freedom to change his religion or belief, and freedom, either alone or in community with others and in public or private, to manifest his religion or belief in teaching, practice, worship and observance.

ARTICLE 19

Everyone has the right to freedom of opinion and expression; this right includes freedom to hold opinions without interference and to seek, receive and impart information and ideas through any media and regardless of frontiers.

ARTICLE 20

(1) Everyone has the right to freedom of peaceful assembly and association.

(2) No one may be compelled to belong to an association.

ARTICLE 21

(1) Everyone has the right to take part in the government of his country, directly or through freely chosen representatives.

(2) Everyone has the right to equal access to public service in his country.

(3) The will of the people shall be the basis of the authority of government; this will shall be expressed in periodic and genuine elections which shall be by universal and equal suffrage and shall be held by secret vote or by equivalent free voting procedures.

ARTICLE 22

Everyone, as a member of society, has the right to social security and is entitled to realization, through national effort and international co-operation and in accordance with the organization and resources of each State, of the economic, social and cultural rights indispensable for his dignity and the free development of his personality.

ARTICLE 23

(1) Everyone has the right to work, to free choice of employment, to just and favourable conditions of work and to protection against unemployment.

(2) Everyone, without any discrimination, has the right to equal pay for equal work.

(3) Everyone who works has the right to just and favourable remuneration ensuring for himself and his family an existence worthy of human dignity, and supplemented, if necessary, by other means of social protection.

(4) Everyone has the right to form and to join trade unions for the protection of his interest.

ARTICLE 24

Everyone has the right to rest and leisure, including reasonable limitation of working hours and periodic holidays with pay.

ARTICLE 25

(1) Everyone has the right to a standard of living adequate for the health and well-being of himself and of his family, including food, clothing, housing and medical care and necessary social services, and the right to security in the event of unemployment, sickness, disability, widowhood, old age or other lack of livelihood in circumstances beyond his control.

(2) Motherhood and childhood are entitled to special care and assistance. All children, whether born in or out of wedlock, shall enjoy the same social protection.

ARTICLE 26

(1) Everyone has the right to education. Education shall be free, at least in the elementary and fundamental stages. Elementary education shall be compulsory. Technical and professional education shall be made generally available and higher education shall be equally accessible to all on the basis of merit.

(2) Education shall be directed to the full development of the human personality and to the strengthening of respect for human rights and fundamental freedoms. It shall promote understanding, tolerance and friendship among all nations, racial or religious groups, and shall further the activities of the United Nations for the maintenance of peace.

(3) Parents have a prior right to choose the kind of education that shall be given to their children.

ARTICLE 27

(1) Everyone has the right freely to participate in the cultural life of the community, to enjoy the arts and to share in scientific advancement and its benefits.

(2) Everyone has the right to the protection of the moral and material interests resulting from any scientific, literary or artistic production of which he is the author.

ARTICLE 28

Everyone is entitled to a social and international order in which the rights and freedoms set forth in this Declaration can be fully realized.

ARTICLE 29

(1) Everyone has duties to the community in which alone the free and full development of his personality is possible.

(2) In the exercise of his rights and freedoms, everyone shall be subject only to such limitations as are determined by law solely for the purpose of securing due recognition and respect for the rights and freedoms of others and of meeting the just requirements of morality, public order and the general welfare in a democratic society.

(3) These rights and freedoms may in no case be exercised contrary to the purposes and principles of the United Nations.

ARTICLE 30

Nothing in this Declaration may be interpreted as implying for any State, group or person any right to engage in any activity or to perform any act aimed at the destruction of any of the rights and freedoms set forth herein.

adopted by: *For: 48*   *Abstentions: 8*

DECLARATION OF THE RIGHTS OF THE CHILD

Unanimously adopted on November 20, 1959, by the General Assembly of the United Nations

PREAMBLE

Whereas the peoples of the United Nations have, in the Charter, reaffirmed their faith in fundamental human rights, and in the dignity and worth of the human person, and have determined to promote social progress and better standards of life in larger freedom,

Whereas the United Nations has, in the Universal Declaration of Human Rights, proclaimed that everyone is entitled to all the rights and freedoms set forth therein, without distinction of any kind, such as race, colour, sex, language, religion, political or other opinion, national or social origin, property, birth or other status,

Whereas the child, by reason of his physical and mental immaturity, needs special safeguards and care, including appropriate legal protection, before as well as after birth,

Whereas the need for such special safeguards has been stated in the Geneva Declaration of the Rights of the Child of 1924, and recognized in the Universal Declaration of Human Rights and in the statutes of specialized agencies and international organizations concerned with the welfare of children,

Whereas mankind owes to the child the best it has to give,

Now therefore,

The General Assembly

Proclaims this Declaration of the Rights of the Child to the end that he may have a happy childhood and enjoy for his own good and for the good of society the rights and freedoms herein set forth, and calls upon parents, upon men and women as individuals and upon voluntary organizations, local authorities and national Governments to recognize these rights and strive for their observance by legislative and other measures progressively taken in accordance with the following principles:

PRINCIPLE 1

The child shall enjoy all the rights set forth in this Declaration. All children, without any exception whatsoever, shall be entitled to these rights, without distinction or discrimination on account of race, colour, sex, language, religion, political or other opinion, national or social origin, property, birth or other status, whether of himself or of his family.

PRINCIPLE 2

The child shall enjoy special protection, and shall be given opportunities and facilities, by law and by other means, to enable him to develop physically, mentally, morally, spiritually and socially in a healthy and normal manner and in conditions of freedom and dignity. In the enactment of laws for this purpose the best interests of the child shall be the paramount consideration.

PRINCIPLE 3

The child shall be entitled from his birth to a name and a nationality.

PRINCIPLE 4

The child shall enjoy the benefits of social security. He shall be entitled to grow and develop in health; to this end special care and protection shall be provided both to him and to his mother, including adequate pre-natal and post-natal care. The child shall have the right to adequate nutrition, housing, recreation and medical services.

PRINCIPLE 5

The child who is physically, mentally or socially handicapped shall be given the special treatment, education and care required by his particular condition.

PRINCIPLE 6

The child, for the full and harmonious development of his personality, needs love and understanding. He shall, wherever possible, grow up in the care and under the responsibility of his parents, and in any case in an atmosphere of affection and of moral and material security; a child of tender years shall not, save in exceptional circumstances, be separated from his mother. Society and the public authorities shall have the duty to extend particular care to children without a family and to those without adequate means of support. Payment of State and other assistance towards the maintenance of children of large families is desirable.

PRINCIPLE 7

The child is entitled to receive education, which shall be free and compulsory, at least in the elementary stages. He shall be given an education which will promote his general culture, and enable him on a basis of equal opportunity to develop his abilities, his individual judgement, and his sense of moral and social responsibility, and to become a useful member of society.

The best interests of the child shall be the guiding principle of those responsible for his education and guidance; that responsibility lies in the first place with his parents.

The child shall have full opportunity for play and recreation, which should be directed to the same purposes as education; society and the public authorities shall endeavour to promote the enjoyment of this right.

PRINCIPLE 8

The child shall in all circumstances be among the first to receive protection and relief.

PRINCIPLE 9

The child shall be protected against all forms of neglect, cruelty and exploitation. He shall not be the subject of traffic, in any form.

The child shall not be admitted to employment before an appropriate minimum age; he shall in no case be caused or permitted to engage in any occupation or employment which would prejudice his health or education, or interfere with his physical, mental or moral development.

PRINCIPLE 10

The child shall be protected from practices which may foster racial, religious and any other form of discrimination. He shall be brought up in a spirit of understanding, tolerance, friendship among peoples, peace and universal brotherhood and in full consciousness that his energy and talents should be devoted to the service of his fellow men.

INTERNATIONAL CONVENTION ON THE ELIMINATION OF ALL FORMS OF RACIAL DISCRIMINATION

The States Parties to this Convention.

Considering that the Charter of the United Nations is based on the principles of the dignity and equality inherent in all human beings, and that all Member States have pledged themselves to take joint and separate action in cooperation with the Organization for the achievement of one of the purposes of the United Nations which is to promote and encourage universal respect for and observance of human rights and fundamental freedoms for all without distinction as to race, sex, language or religion,

Considering that the Universal Declaration of Human Rights proclaims that all human beings are born free and equal in dignity and rights and that everyone is entitled to all the rights and freedoms set out therein, without distinctions of any kind, in particular as to race, colour or national origin,

Considering that all human beings are equal before the law and are entitled to equal protection of the law against any discrimination and against any incitement to discrimination,

Considering that the United Nations has condemned colonialism and all practices of segregation and discrimination associated therewith, in whatever form and wherever they exist, and that the Declaration on the Granting of Independence to Colonial Countries and Peoples of 14 December 1960 (General Assembly resolution 1514 [XV]) has affirmed and solemnly proclaimed the necessity of bringing them to a speedy and unconditional end,

Considering that the United Nations Declaration on the Elimination of All Forms of Racial Discrimination of 20 November 1963 (General Assembly resolution 1904 [XVIII]) solemnly affirms the necessity of speedily eliminating racial discrimination throughout the world in all its forms and manifestations and of securing understanding of and respect for the dignity of the human person,

Convinced that any doctrine of superiority based on racial differentiation is scientifically false, morally condemnable, socially unjust and dangerous, and that there is no justification for racial discrimination, in theory or in practice, anywhere,

Reaffirming that discrimination between human beings on the grounds of race, colour or ethnic origin is an obstacle to friendly and peaceful relations among nations and is capable of disturbing peace and security among peoples and the harmony of persons living side by side even within one and the same State,

Convinced that the existence of racial barriers is repugnant to the ideals of any human society,

Alarmed by manifestations of racial discrimination still in evidence in some areas of the world and by governmental policies based on racial superiority or hatred, such as policies of *apartheid*, segregation or separation,

Resolved to adopt all necessary measures for speedily eliminating racial discrimination in all its forms and manifestations and to prevent and combat racist doctrines and practices in order to promote understanding between races and to build an international community free from all forms of racial segregation and racial discrimination,

Bearing in mind the Convention on Discrimination in Respect of Employment and Occupation adopted by the International Labour Organization in 1958, and the Convention Against Discrimination in Education adopted by the United Nations Educational, Scientific and Cultural Organization in 1960,

Desiring to implement the principles embodied in the United Nations Declaration on the Elimination of All Forms of Racial Discrimination and to secure the earliest adoption of practical measures to that end,

Have agreed as follows:

Part I

ARTICLE 1

1. In this Convention the term "racial discrimination" shall mean any distinction, exclusion, restriction or preference based on race, colour, descent, or national or ethnic origin which has the purpose or effect of nullifying or impairing the recognition, enjoyment or exercise, on an equal footing, of human rights and fundamental freedoms in the political, economic, social, cultural or any other field of public life.

2. This Convention shall not apply to distinctions, exclusions, restrictions or preferences made by a State Party to this Convention between citizens and non-citizens.

3. Nothing in this Convention may be interpreted as affecting in any way the legal provisions of States Parties concerning nationality, citizenship or naturalization, provided that such provisions do not discriminate against any particular nationality.

4. Special measures taken for the sole purpose of securing adequate advancement of certain racial or ethnic groups or individuals requiring such protection as may be necessary in order to ensure to such groups or individuals equal enjoyment or exercise of human rights and fundamental freedoms shall not be deemed racial discrimination, provided, however, that such measures do not, as a consequence, lead to the maintenance of separate rights for different racial groups and that they shall not be continued after the objectives for which they were taken have been achieved.

ARTICLE 2

7. States Parties condemn racial discrimination and undertake to pursue by all appropriate means and without delay a policy of eliminating racial discrimination in all its forms, and promoting understanding among all races, and to this end:

(*a*) Each State Party undertakes to engage in no act or practice of racial discrimination against persons, groups of persons or institutions and to ensure that all public authorities and public institutions, national and local, shall act in conformity with this obligation;

(*b*) Each State Party undertakes not to sponsor, defend or support racial discrimination by any persons or organizations;

(*c*) Each State Party shall take effective measures to review governmental, national and local policies, and to amend, rescind or nullify any laws and regulations which have the effect of creating or perpetuating racial discrimination wherever it exists;

(*d*) Each State Party shall prohibit and bring to an end, by all appropriate means, including legislation as required by circumstances, racial discrimination by any persons, group or organization;

(*e*) Each State Party undertakes to encourage, where appropriate, integrationist multi-racial organizations and movements and other means of eliminating barriers between races, and to discourage anything which tends to strengthen racial division.

2. States Parties shall, when the circumstances so warrant, take, in the social, economic, cultural and other fields, special and concrete measures to ensure the adequate development and protection of certain racial groups or individuals belonging to them for the purpose of guaranteeing them the full and equal enjoyment of human rights and fundamental freedoms. These measures shall in no case entail as a consequence the maintenance of unequal or separate rights for different racial groups after the objectives for which they were taken have been achieved.

ARTICLE 3

States Parties particularly condemn racial segregation and *apartheid* and undertake to prevent, prohibit and eradicate, in territories under their jurisdiction, all practices of this nature.

ARTICLE 4

States Parties condemn all propaganda and all organizations which are based on ideas or theories of superiority of one race or group of persons of one colour or ethnic origin, or which attempt to justify or promote racial hatred and discrimination in any form, and undertake to adopt immediate and positive measures designed to eradicate all incitement to, or acts of, such discrimination, and to this end, with due regard to the principles embodied in the Universal Declaration of Human Rights and the rights expressly set forth in Article 5 of this Convention, *inter alia*:

(*a*) Shall declare an offense punishable by law all dissemination of ideas based on racial superiority or hatred, incitement to racial discrimination, as well as all acts of violence or incitement to such acts against any race or group of persons of another colour or ethnic origin, and also the provision of any assistance to racist activities, including the financing thereof;

(*b*) Shall declare illegal and prohibit organizations, and also organized and all other propaganda activities, which promote and incite racial discrimination, and shall recognize participation in such organizations or activities as an offense punishable by law;

(*c*) Shall not permit public authorities or public institutions, national, or local, to promote or incite racial discrimination.

ARTICLE 5

In compliance with the fundamental obligations laid down in Article 2, States Parties undertake to prohibit and to eliminate racial discrimination in all its forms and to guarantee the right of everyone, without distinction as to race, colour, or national or ethnic origin, to equality before the law, notably in the enjoyment of the following rights:

(*a*) The right to equal treatment before the tribunals and all other organs administering justice;

(*b*) The right to security of person and protection by the State against violence or bodily harm, whether inflicted by government officials or by any individual, group or institution;

(*c*) Political rights, in particular the rights to participate in elections, to vote and to stand for election—on the basis of universal and equal suffrage, to take part in the government, as well as in the conduct of public affairs at any level and to have equal access to public service;

(*d*) Other civil rights, in particular;

(i) the right to freedom of movement and residence within the border of the State;

(ii) the right to leave any country, including his own, and to return to his country;

(iii) the right to nationality;

(iv) the right to marriage and choice of spouse;

(v) the right to own property alone, as well as in association with others;

(vi) the right to inherit;

(vii) the right to freedom of thought, conscience and religion;

(viii) the right to freedom of opinion and expression;

(ix) the right to freedom of peaceful assembly and association;

(e) Economic, social and cultural rights, in particular:

(i) the rights to work, free choice of employment, just and favourable conditions of work, protection against unemployment, equal pay for equal work, just and favourable remuneration;

(ii) the right to form and join trade unions;

(iii) the right to housing;

(iv) the right to public health, medical care and social security and social services;

(v) the right to education and training;

(vi) the right to equal participation in cultural activities;

(f) The right of access to any place or service intended for use by the general public such as transport, hotels, restaurants, cafes, theatres, parks.

ARTICLE 6

States Parties shall assure to everyone within their jurisdiction effective protection and remedies through the competent national tribunals and other State institutions against any acts of racial discrimination which violate his human rights and fundamental freedoms contrary to this Convention, as well as the right to seek from such tribunals just and adequate reparation or satisfaction for any damage suffered as a result of such discrimination.

ARTICLE 7

States Parties undertake to adopt immediate and effective measures, particularly in the fields of teaching, education, culture and information, with a view to combating prejudices which lead to racial discrimination and to promoting understanding, tolerance and friendship among nations and racial or ethnic groups, as well as to propagating the purposes and principles of the Charter of the United Nations, the Universal Declaration of Human Rights, the United Nations Declaration on the Elimination of All Forms of Racial Discrimination, and this Convention.

Part II

ARTICLE 8

1. There shall be established a Committee on the Elimination of Racial Discrimination (hereinafter referred to as the Committee) consisting of eighteen experts of high moral standing and acknowledged impartiality elected by States Parties from amongst their nationals who shall serve in their personal capacity, consideration being given to equitable geographical distribution and to the representation of the different forms of civilization, as well as of the principal legal systems.

2. The members of the Committee shall be elected by secret ballot from a list of persons nominated by the States Parties. Each State Party may nominate one person from among its own nationals.

3. The initial election shall be held six months after the date of the entry into force of this Convention. At least three months before the date of each election the Secretary-General of the United Nations shall address a letter to the States Parties inviting them to submit their nominations within two months. The Secretary-General shall prepare a list in alphabetical order of all persons thus nominated indicating the States Parties which have nominated them and shall submit it to the States Parties.

4. Elections of the members of the Committee shall be held at a meeting of States Parties convened by the Secretary-General at the Headquarters of the United Nations. At that meeting, for which two-thirds of the States Parties shall constitute a quorum, the persons elected to the Committee shall be those nominees who obtain the largest number of votes and an absolute majority of the votes of the representatives of States Parties present and voting.

5. (a) The members of the Committee shall be elected for a term of four years. However, the terms of nine of the members elected at the first election shall expire at the end of two years; immediately after

the first election the names of these nine members shall be chosen by lot by the Chairman of the Committee.

(*b*) For the filling of casual vacancies, the State Party whose expert has ceased to function as a member of the Committee shall appoint another expert from among its nationals subject to the approval of the Committee.

6. The States Parties shall be responsible for the expenses of the members of the Committee while they are in performance of Committee duties.

ARTICLE 9

1. The States Parties undertake to submit to the Secretary-General for consideration by the Committee a report on the legislative, judicial, administrative, or other measures that they have adopted and that give effect to the provisions of this Convention: (*a*) within one year after the entry into force of the Convention for the State concerned; and (*b*) thereafter every two years and whenever the Committee so requests. The Committee may request further information from the States Parties.

2. The Committee shall report annually through the Secretary-General to the General Assembly on its activities and may make suggestions and general recommendations based on the examination of the reports and information received from the States Parties. Such suggestions and general recommendations shall be reported to the General Assembly together with comments, if any, from States Parties.

ARTICLE 10

1. The Committee shall adopt its own rules of procedure.

2. The Committee shall elect its officers for a term of two years.

3. The secretariat of the Committee shall be provided by the Secretary-General of the United Nations.

4. The meetings of the Committee shall normally be held at the Headquarters of the United Nations.

ARTICLE 11

1. If a State Party considers that another State Party is not giving effect to the provisions of this Convention, it may bring the matter to

the attention of the Committee. The Committee shall then transmit the communication to the State Party concerned. Within three months, the receiving State shall submit to the Committee written explanations or statements clarifying the matter and the remedy, if any, that may have been taken by that State.

2. If the matter is not adjusted to the satisfaction of both parties, either by bilateral negotiations or by any other procedure open to them, within six months after the receipt by the receiving State of the initial communication, either State shall have the right to refer the matter again to the Committee by notice given to the Committee and also to the other State.

3. The Committee shall deal with a matter referred to it in accordance with paragraph 2 of this article after it has ascertained that all available domestic remedies have been invoked and exhausted in the case, in conformity with the generally recognized principles of international law. This shall not be the rule where the application of the remedies is unreasonably prolonged.

4. In any matter referred to it, the Committee may call upon the States Parties concerned to supply any other relevant information.

5. When any matter arising out of this article is being considered by the Committee, the States Parties concerned shall be entitled to send a representative to take part in the proceedings of the Committee, without voting rights, while the matter is under consideration.

ARTICLE 12

1. (*a*) After the Committee has obtained and collated all the information it thinks necessary, the Chairman shall appoint an *ad hoc* Conciliation Commission (hereinafter referred to as the Commission) comprising five persons who may or may not be members of the Committee. The members of the Commission shall be appointed with the unanimous consent of the parties to the dispute, and its good offices shall be made available to the States concerned with a view to an amicable solution to the matter on the basis of respect for this Convention.

(*b*) If the States Parties to the dispute fail to reach agreement on all or part of the composition of the Commission within three months, the members of the Commission not agreed upon by the States Parties to the dispute shall be elected by two-thirds majority vote by secret ballot of the Committee from among its own members.

2. The members of the Commission shall serve in their personal capacity. They shall not be nationals of the States Parties to the dispute or of a State not Party to this Convention.

3. The Commission shall elect its own Chairman and adopt its own rules of procedure.

4. The meetings of the Commission shall normally be held at the Headquarters of the United Nations, or at any other convenient place as determined by the Commission.

5. The secretariat provided in accordance with article 10, paragraph 3, shall also service the Commission whenever a dispute among States Parties brings the Commission into being.

6. The States Parties to the dispute shall share equally all the expenses of the members of the Commission in accordance with estimates to be provided by the Secretary-General.

7. The Secretary-General shall be empowered to pay the expenses of the members of the Commission, if necessary, before reimbursement by the States Parties to the dispute in accordance with paragraph 6 of this article.

8. The information obtained and collated by the Committee shall be made available to the Commission and the Commission may call upon the States concerned to supply any other relevant information.

ARTICLE 13

1. When the Commission has fully considered the matter, it shall prepare and submit to the Chairman of the Committee a report embodying its findings on all questions of fact relevant to the issue between the parties and containing such recommendations as it may think proper for the amicable solution of the dispute.

2. The Chairman of the Committee shall communicate the report of the Commission to each of the States Parties to the dispute. These States shall within three months inform the Chairman of the Committee whether or not they accept the recommendations contained in the report of the Commission.

3. After the period provided for in paragraph 2 of this article, the

Chairman of the Committee shall communicate the report of the Commission and the declarations of States Parties concerned to the other States Parties to this Convention.

ARTICLE 14

1. A State Party may at any time declare that it recognizes the competence of the Committee to receive and consider communications from individuals or groups of individuals within its jurisdiction claiming to be victims of a violation by that State Party of any of the rights set forth in this Convention. No communication shall be received by the Committee if it concerns a State Party which has not made such a declaration.

2. Any State Party which makes a declaration as provided for in paragraph 1 of this article may establish or indicate a body within its national legal order which shall be competent to receive and consider petitions from individuals and groups of individuals within its jurisdiction who claim to be victims of a violation of any of the rights set forth in this Convention and who have exhausted other available local remedies.

3. A declaration made in accordance with paragraph 1 of this article and the name of any body established or indicated in accordance with paragraph 2 of this article, shall be deposited by the State Party concerned with the Secretary-General of the United Nations, who shall transmit copies thereof to the other State Parties. A declaration may be withdrawn at any time by notification to the Secretary-General, but such a withdrawal shall not affect communications pending before the Committee.

4. A register of petitions shall be kept by the body established or indicated in accordance with paragraph 2 of this article, and certified copies of the register shall be filed annually through appropriate channels with the Secretary-General on the understanding that the contents shall not be publicly disclosed.

5. In the event of failure to obtain satisfaction from the body established or indicated in accordance with paragraph 2 of this article, the petitioner shall have the right to communicate the matter to the Committee within six months.

6. (*a*) The Committee shall confidentially bring any communica-

tion referred to it to the attention of the State Party alleged to be violating any provision of this Convention, but the identity of the individual or groups of individuals concerned shall not be revealed without his or their express consent. The Committee shall not receive anonymous communications.

(b) Within three months, the receiving State shall submit to the Committee written explanations or statements clarifying the matter and the remedy, if any, that may have been taken by that State.

7. (a) The Committee shall consider communications in the light of all information made available to it by the State Party concerned and by the petitioner. The Committee shall not consider any communication from a petitioner unless it has ascertained that the petitioner has exhausted all available domestic remedies. However, this shall not be the rule where the application of the remedies is unreasonably prolonged.

(b) The Committee shall forward its suggestions and recommendations, if any, to the State Party concerned and to the petitioner.

8. The Committee shall include in its annual report a summary of such communications and, where appropriate, summary of the explanations and statements of the States Parties concerned and of its own suggestions and recommendations.

9. The Committee shall be competent to exercise the functions provided for in this article only when at least ten States Parties to this Convention are bound by declarations in accordance with paragraph 1 of this article.

ARTICLE 15

1. Pending the achievement of the objectives of General Assembly resolution 1514 (XV) of 14 December 1960 concerning the Declaration on the Granting of Independence to Colonial Countries and Peoples, the provisions of this Convention shall in no way limit the right of petition granted to these peoples by other international instruments or by the United Nations and its specialized agencies.

2. (a) The Committee established under article 8, paragraph 1, shall receive copies of the petitions from, and submit expressions of opinion and recommendations on these petitions to, the bodies of the

United Nations which deal with matters directly related to the principles and objectives of this Convention in their consideration of petitions from the inhabitants of Trust and Non-Self-Governing Territories, and all other territories to which General Assembly resolution 1514 (XV) applies, relating to matters covered by this Convention which are before these bodies.

(*b*) The Committee shall receive from the competent bodies of the United Nations copies of the reports concerning the legislative, judicial, administrative or other measures directly related to the principles and objectives of this Convention applied by the administering Powers within the territories mentioned in subparagraph (*a*) of this paragraph and shall express opinions and make recommendations to these bodies.

3. The Committee shall include in its report to the General Assembly a summary of the petitions and reports it has received from United Nations bodies, and the expressions of opinion and recommendations of the Committee related to the said petitions and reports.

4. The Committee shall request from the Secretary-General of the United Nations all information relevant to the objectives of this Convention and available to him regarding the territories mentioned in paragraph 2 (*a*) of this article.

ARTICLE 16

The provisions of this Convention concerning the settlement of disputes or complaints shall be applied without prejudice to other procedures for settling disputes or complaints in the field of discrimination laid down in the constituent instruments of, or in conventions adopted by, the United Nations and its specialized agencies, and shall not prevent the States Parties from having recourse to other procedures for settling a dispute in accordance with general or special international agreements in force between them.

Part III

ARTICLE 17

1. This Convention is open for signature by any State Member of the United Nations or member of any of its specialized agencies, by

any State Party to the Statute of the International Court of Justice, and by any other State which has been invited by the General Assembly of the United Nations to become a Party to this Convention.

2. This Convention is subject to ratification. Instruments of ratification shall be deposited with the Secretary-General of the United Nations.

ARTICLE 18

1. This Convention shall be open to accession by any State referred to in article 17, paragraph 1.

2. Accession shall be effected by the deposit of any instrument of accession with the Secretary-General of the United Nations.

ARTICLE 19

1. This Convention shall enter into force on the thirtieth day after the date of the deposit with the Secretary-General of the United Nations of the twenty-seventh instrument of ratification or instrument of accession.

2. For each State ratifying this Convention or acceding to it after the deposit of the twenty-seventh instrument of ratification or instrument of accession, the Convention shall enter into force on the thirtieth day after the date of the deposit of its own instrument of ratification or instrument of accession.

ARTICLE 20

1. The Secretary-General of the United Nations shall receive and circulate to all States which are or may become parties to this Convention reservations made by States at the time of ratification or accession. Any State which objects to the reservation shall, within a period of ninety days from the date of the said communication, notify the Secretary-General that it does not accept it.

2. A reservation incompatible with the object and purpose of this Convention shall not be permitted, nor shall a reservation, the effect of which would inhibit the operation of any of the bodies established by the Convention, be allowed. A reservation shall be considered incom-

patible or inhibitive if at least two-thirds of the States Parties to the Convention object to it.

3. Reservations may be withdrawn at any time by notification to this effect addressed to the Secretary-General. Such notification shall take effect on the date on which it is received.

ARTICLE 21

A State Party may denounce this Convention by written notification to the Secretary-General of the United Nations. Denunciation shall take effect one year after the date of receipt of the notification by the Secretary-General.

ARTICLE 22

Any dispute between two or more States Parties over the interpretation or application of this Convention, which is not settled by negotiation or by the procedures expressly provided for in this Convention, shall at the request of any of the parties to the dispute be referred to the International Court of Justice for decision, unless the disputants agree to another mode of settlement.

ARTICLE 23

1. A request for the revision of this Convention may be made at any time by the State Party by means of a notification in writing addressed to the Secretary-General.

2. The General Assembly shall decide upon the steps, if any, to be taken in respect of such a request.

ARTICLE 24

The Secretary-General of the United Nations shall inform all States referred to in article 17, paragraph 1, of the following particulars:

(*a*) Signatures, ratifications and accessions under articles 17 and 18;

(*b*) The date of entry into force of this Convention under article 19;

(*c*) Communications and declarations received under articles 14 and 22;

(*d*) Denunciation under article 20.

ARTICLE 25

1. This Convention, of which the Chinese, English, French, Russian and Spanish texts are equally authentic, shall be deposited in the archives of the United Nations.

2. The Secretary-General of the United Nations shall transmit certified copies of this Convention to all States belonging to any of the categories mentioned in article 17, paragraph 1.

(Total number of States Parties: 97)

The International Covenants on Human Rights and Optional Protocol

INTERNATIONAL COVENANT ON ECONOMIC, SOCIAL AND CULTURAL RIGHTS

The States Parties to the Present Covenant,

Considering that, in accordance with the principles proclaimed in the Charter of the United Nations, recognition of the inherent dignity and of the equal and inalienable rights of all members of the human family is the foundation of freedom, justice and peace in the world.

Recognizing that these rights derive from the inherent dignity of the human person,

Recognizing that, in accordance with the Universal Declaration of Human Rights, the ideal of free human beings enjoying freedom from fear and want can only be achieved if conditions are created whereby everyone may enjoy his economic, social and cultural rights, as well as his civil and political rights,

Considering the obligation of States under the Charter of the United Nations to promote universal respect for, and observance of, human rights and freedoms,

Realizing that the individual, having duties to other individuals and to the community to which he belongs, is under a responsibility to strive for the promotion and observance of the rights recognized in the present Covenant,

Agree upon the following articles:

Part 1

ARTICLE 1

1. All peoples have the right of self-determination. By virtue of that right they freely determine their political status and freely pursue their economic, social and cultural development.

2. All peoples may, for their own ends, freely dispose of their natural wealth and resources without prejudice to any obligations arising out of international economic co-operation, based upon the principle of mutual benefit, and international law. In no case may a people be deprived of its own means of subsistence.

3. The States Parties to the present Covenant, including those having responsibility for the administration of Non-Self-Governing and Trust Territories, shall promote the realization of the right of self-determination, and shall respect that right, in conformity with the provisions of the Charter of the United Nations.

Part 2

ARTICLE 2

1. Each State Party to the present Covenant undertakes to take steps, individually and through international assistance and co-operation, especially economic and technical, to the maximum of its available resources, with a view to achieving progressively the full realization of the rights recognized in the present Covenant by all appropriate means, including particularly the adoption of legislative measures.

2. The States Parties to the present Covenant undertake to guarantee that the rights enunciated in the present Covenant will be exercised without discrimination of any kind as to race, colour, sex, language, religion, political or other opinion, national or social origin, property, birth or other status.

3. Developing countries, with due regard to human rights and their national economy, may determine to what extent they would guarantee the economic rights recognized in the present Covenant to non-nationals.

ARTICLE 3

The States Parties to the present Covenant undertake to ensure the equal right of men and women to the enjoyment of all economic, social and cultural rights set forth in the present Covenant.

ARTICLE 4

The States Parties to the present Covenant recognize that, in the enjoyment of those rights provided by the State in conformity with the present Covenant, the State may subject such rights only to such limitations as are determined by law only in so far as this may be compatible with the nature of these rights and solely for the purpose of promoting the general welfare in a democratic society.

ARTICLE 5

1. Nothing in the present Covenant may be interpreted as implying for any State, group or person any right to engage in any activity or to perform any act aimed at the destruction of any of the rights or freedoms recognized herein, or at their limitation to a greater extent than is provided for in the present Covenant.

2. No restriction upon or derogation from any of the fundamental human rights recognized or existing in any country in virtue of law, conventions, regulations or custom shall be admitted on the pretext that the present Covenant does not recognize such rights or that it recognizes them to a lesser extent.

Part 3

ARTICLE 6

1. The States Parties to the present Covenant recognize the right to work, which includes the right of everyone to the opportunity to gain his living by work which he freely chooses or accepts, and will take appropriate steps to safeguard this right.

2. The steps to be taken by a State Party to the present Covenant to achieve the full realization of this right shall include technical and vocational guidance and training programmes, policies and techniques to achieve steady economic, social and cultural development and full

and productive employment under conditions safeguarding fundamental political and economic freedoms to the individual.

ARTICLE 7

The States Parties to the present Covenant recognize the right of everyone to the enjoyment of just and favourable conditions of work which ensure, in particular:

(*a*) Remuneration which provides all workers, as a minimum, with:

(i) Fair wages and equal remuneration for work of equal value without distinction of any kind, in particular women being guaranteed conditions of work not inferior to those enjoyed by men, with equal pay for equal work;

(ii) A decent living for themselves and their families in accordance with the provisions of the present Covenant;

(*b*) Safe and healthy working conditions;

(*c*) Equal opportunity for everyone to be promoted in his employment to an appropriate higher level, subject to no considerations other than those of seniority and competence;

(*d*) Rest, leisure and reasonable limitation of working hours and periodic holidays with pay, as well as remuneration for public holidays.

ARTICLE 8

1. The States Parties to the present Covenant undertake to ensure:

(*a*) The right of everyone to form trade unions and join the trade union of his choice, subject only to the rules of the organization concerned, for the promotion and protection of his economic and social interests. No restrictions may be placed on the exercise of this right other than those prescribed by law and which are necessary in a democratic society in the interests of national security or public order or for the protection of the rights and freedoms of others;

(*b*) The right of trade unions to establish national federations or confederations and the right of the latter to form or join international trade-union organizations;

(*c*) The right of trade unions to function freely subject to no limitations other than those prescribed by law and which are necessary in a democratic society in the interests of national security or public order or for the protection of the rights and freedoms of others;

(*d*) The right to strike, provided that it is exercised in conformity with the laws of the particular country.

2. This article shall not prevent the imposition of lawful restrictions on the exercise of these rights by members of the armed forces or of the police or of the administration of the State.

3. Nothing in this article shall authorize States Parties to the International Labour Organisation Convention of 1948 concerning Freedom of Association and Protection of the Right to Organize to take legislative measures which would prejudice, or apply the law in such a manner as would prejudice, the guarantees provided for in that Convention.

ARTICLE 9

The States Parties to the present Covenant recognize the right of everyone to social security, including social insurance.

ARTICLE 10

The States Parties to the present Covenant recognize that:

1. The widest possible protection and assistance should be accorded to the family, which is the natural and fundamental group unit of society, particularly for its establishment and while it is responsible for the care and education of dependent children. Marriage must be entered into with the free consent of the intending spouses.

2. Special protection should be accorded to mothers during a reasonable period before and after childbirth. During such period working mothers should be accorded paid leave or leave with adequate social security benefits.

3. Special measures of protection and assistance should be taken on behalf of all children and young persons without any discrimination for reasons of parentage or other conditions. Children and young persons should be protected from economic and social exploitation. Their employment in work harmful to their morals or health or dangerous to life or likely to hamper their normal development should be punishable by law. States should also set age limits below which the

paid employment of child labour should be prohibited and punishable by law.

ARTICLE 11

1. The States Parties to the present Covenant recognize the right of everyone to an adequate standard of living for himself and his family, including adequate food, clothing and housing, and to the continuous improvement of living conditions. The States Parties will take appropriate steps to ensure the realization of this right, recognizing to this effect the essential importance of international co-operation based on free consent.

2. The States Parties to the present Covenant, recognizing the fundamental right of everyone to be free from hunger, shall take, individually and through international co-operation, the measures, including specific programmes, which are needed:

(a) To improve methods of production, conservation and distribution of food by making full use of technical and scientific knowledge, by disseminating knowledge of the principles of nutrition and by developing or reforming agrarian systems in such a way as to achieve the most efficient development and utilization of natural resources;

(b) Taking into account the problems of both food-importing and food-exporting countries, to ensure an equitable distribution of world food supplies in relation to need.

ARTICLE 12

1. The States Parties to the present Covenant recognize the right of everyone to the enjoyment of the highest attainable standard of physical and mental health.

2. The steps to be taken by the States Parties to the present Covenant to achieve the full realization of this right shall include those necessary for:

(a) The provision for the reduction of the stillbirth-rate and of infant mortality and for the healthy development of the child;

(b) The improvement of all aspects of environmental and industrial hygiene;

(*c*) The prevention, treatment and control of epidemic, endemic, occupational and other diseases;

(*d*) The creation of conditions which would assure to all medical service and medical attention in the event of sickness.

ARTICLE 13

1. The States Parties to the present Covenant recognize the right of everyone to education. They agree that education shall be directed to the full development of the human personality and the sense of its dignity, and shall strengthen the respect for human rights and fundamental freedoms. They further agree that education shall enable all persons to participate effectively in a free society, promote understanding, tolerance and friendship among all nations and all racial, ethnic or religious groups, and further the activities of the United Nations for the maintenance of peace.

2. The States Parties to the present Covenant recognize that, with a view to achieving the full realization of this right:

(*a*) Primary education shall be compulsory and available free to all;

(*b*) Secondary education in its different forms, including technical and vocational secondary education, shall be made generally available and accessible to all by every appropriate means, and in particular by the progressive introduction of free education;

(*c*) Higher education shall be made equally accessible to all, on the basis of capacity, by every appropriate means, and in particular by the progressive introduction of free education;

(*d*) Fundamental education shall be encouraged or intensified as far as possible for those persons who have not received or completed the whole period of their primary education;

(*e*) The development of a system of schools at all levels shall be actively pursued, an adequate fellowship system shall be established, and the material conditions of teaching staff shall be continuously improved.

3. The States Parties to the present Covenant undertake to have respect for the liberty of parents and, when applicable, legal guardians to choose for their children schools, other than those established by the public authorities, which conform to such minimum educational

standards as may be laid down or approved by the State and to ensure the religious and moral education of their children in conformity with their own convictions.

4. No part of this article shall be construed so as to interfere with the liberty of individuals and bodies to establish and direct educational institutions, subject always to the observance of the principles set forth in paragraph 1 of this article and to the requirement that the education given in such institutions shall conform to such minimum standards as may be laid down by the State.

ARTICLE 14

Each State Party to the present Covenant which, at the time of becoming a Party, has not been able to secure in its metropolitan territory or other territories under its jurisdiction compulsory primary education, free of charge, undertakes, within two years, to work out and adopt a detailed plan of action for the progressive implementation, within a reasonable number of years, to be fixed in the plan, of the principle of compulsory education free of charge for all.

ARTICLE 15

1. The States Parties to the present Covenant recognize the right of everyone:

(a) To take part in cultural life;

(b) To enjoy the benefits of scientific progress and its applications;

(c) To benefit from the protection of the moral and material interests resulting from any scientific, literary or artistic production of which he is the author.

2. The steps to be taken by the States Parties to the present Covenant to achieve the full realization of this right shall include those necessary for the conservation, the development and the diffusion of science and culture.

3. The States Parties to the present Covenant undertake to respect the freedom indispensable for scientific research and creative activity.

4. The States Parties to the present Covenant recognize the benefits to be derived from the encouragement and development of international contacts and co-operation in the scientific and cultural fields.

Part 4

ARTICLE 16

1. The States Parties to the present Covenant undertake to submit in conformity with this part of the Covenant reports on the measures which they have adopted and the progress made in achieving the observance of the rights recognized herein.

2. (*a*) All reports shall be submitted to the Secretary-General of the United Nations, who shall transmit copies to the Economic and Social Council for consideration in accordance with the provisions of the present Covenant.

(*b*) The Secretary-General of the United Nations shall also transmit to the specialized agencies copies of the reports, or any relevant parts therefrom, from States Parties to the present Covenant which are also members of these specialized agencies in so far as these reports, or parts therefrom, relate to any matters which fall within the responsibilities of the said agencies in accordance with their constitutional instruments.

ARTICLE 17

1. The States Parties to the present Covenant shall furnish their reports in stages, in accordance with a programme to be established by the Economic and Social Council within one year of the entry into force of the present Covenant after consultation with the States Parties and the specialized agencies concerned.

2. Reports may indicate factors and difficulties affecting the degree of fulfillment of obligations under the present Covenant.

3. Where relevant information has previously been furnished to the United Nations or to any specialized agency by any State Party to the present Covenant, it will not be necessary to reproduce that information, but a precise reference to the information so furnished will suffice.

ARTICLE 18

Pursuant to its responsibilities under the Charter of the United Nations in the field of human rights and fundamental freedoms, the Economic and Social Council may make arrangements with the specialized agencies in respect of their reporting to it on the progress made in achieving the observance of the provisions of the present Covenant falling within the scope of their activities. These reports may include particulars of decisions and recommendations on such implementation adopted by their competent organs.

ARTICLE 19

The Economic and Social Council may transmit to the Commission on Human Rights for study and general recommendation or, as appropriate, for information the reports concerning human rights submitted by States in accordance with articles 16 and 17, and those concerning human rights submitted by the specialized agencies in accordance with article 18.

ARTICLE 20

The States Parties to the present Covenant and the specialized agencies concerned may submit comments to the Economic and Social Council on any general recommendation under article 19 or reference to such general recommendation in any report of the Commission on Human Rights or any documentation referred to therein.

ARTICLE 21

The Economic and Social Council may submit from time to time to the General Assembly reports with recommendations of a general nature and a summary of the information received from the States Parties to the present Covenant and the specialized agencies on the measures taken and the progress made in achieving general observance of the rights recognized in the present Covenant.

ARTICLE 22

The Economic and Social Council may bring to the attention of other organs of the United Nations, their subsidiary organs and specialized agencies concerned with furnishing technical assistance any matters arising out of the reports referred to in this part of the present Covenant which may assist such bodies in deciding, each within its field of competence, on the advisability of international measures likely to contribute to the effective progressive implementation of the present Covenant.

ARTICLE 23

The States Parties to the present Covenant agree that international action for the achievement of the rights recognized in the present Covenant includes such methods as the conclusion of conventions, the adoption of recommendations, the furnishing of technical assistance and the holding of regional meetings and technical meetings for the purpose of consultation and study organized in conjunction with the Governments concerned.

ARTICLE 24

Nothing in the present Covenant shall be interpreted as impairing the provisions of the Charter of the United Nations and of the constitutions of the specialized agencies which define the respective responsibilities of the various organs of the United Nations and of the specialized agencies in regard to the matters dealt with in the present Covenant.

ARTICLE 25

Nothing in the present Covenant shall be interpreted as impairing the inherent right of all peoples to enjoy and utilize fully and freely their natural wealth and resources.

Part 5

ARTICLE 26

1. The present Covenant is open for signature by any State Member of the United Nations or member of any of its specialized agencies, by any State Party to the Statute of the International Court of Justice, and by any other State which has been invited by the General Assembly of the United Nations to become a party to the present Covenant.

2. The present Covenant is subject to ratification. Instruments of ratification shall be deposited with the Secretary-General of the United Nations.

3. The present Covenant shall be open to accession by any State referred to in paragraph 1 of this article.

4. Accession shall be effected by the deposit of an instrument of accession with the Secretary-General of the United Nations.

5. The Secretary-General of the United Nations shall inform all States which have signed the present Covenant or acceded to it of the deposit of each instrument of ratification or accession.

ARTICLE 27

1. The present Covenant shall enter into force three months after the date of the deposit with the Secretary-General of the United Nations of the thirty-fifth instrument of ratification or instrument of accession.

2. For each State ratifying the present Covenant or acceding to it after the deposit of the thirty-fifth instrument of ratification or instrument of accession, the present Covenant shall enter into force three months after the date of the deposit of its own instrument of ratification or instrument of accession.

ARTICLE 28

The provisions of the present Covenant shall extend to all parts of federal States without any limitation or exceptions.

ARTICLE 29

1. Any State Party to the present Covenant may propose an amendment and file it with the Secretary-General of the United Nations. The Secretary-General shall thereupon communicate any proposed amendments to the States Parties to the present Covenant with a request that they notify him whether they favour a conference of States Parties for the purpose of considering and voting upon the proposals. In the event that at least one-third of the States Parties favours such a conference, the Secretary-General shall convene the conference under the auspices of the United Nations. Any amendment adopted by a majority of the States Parties present and voting at the conference shall be submitted to the General Assembly of the United Nations for approval.

2. Amendments shall come into force when they have been approved by the General Assembly of the United Nations and accepted by a two-thirds majority of the States Parties to the present Covenant in accordance with their respective constitutional processes.

3. When amendments come into force they shall be binding on those States Parties which have accepted them, other States Parties still being bound by the provisions of the present Covenant and any earlier amendment which they have accepted.

ARTICLE 30

Irrespective of the notifications made under article 26, paragraph 5, the Secretary-General of the United Nations shall inform all States referred to in paragraph 1 of the same article of the following particulars:

(*a*) Signatures, ratifications and accessions under article 26;

(*b*) The date of the entry into force of the present Covenant under article 27 and the date of the entry into force of any amendments under article 29.

ARTICLE 31

1. The present Covenant, of which the Chinese, English, French, Russian and Spanish texts are equally authentic, shall be deposited in the archives of the United Nations.

2. The Secretary-General of the United Nations shall transmit certified copies of the present Covenant to all States referred to in article 26.

INTERNATIONAL COVENANT ON CIVIL AND POLITICAL RIGHTS

The States Parties to the present Covenant,

Considering that, in accordance with the principles proclaimed in the Charter of the United Nations, recognition of the inherent dignity and of the equal and inalienable rights of all members of the human family is the foundation of freedom, justice and peace in the world,

Recognizing that these rights derive from the inherent dignity of the human person,

Recognizing that, in accordance with the Universal Declaration of Human Rights, the ideal of free human beings enjoying civil and political freedom and freedom from fear and want can only be achieved if conditions are created whereby everyone may enjoy his civil and political rights, as well as his economic, social and cultural rights,

Considering the obligation of States under the Charter of the United Nations to promote universal respect for, and observance of, human rights and freedoms,

Realizing that the individual, having duties to other individuals and to the community to which he belongs, is under a responsibility to strive for the promotion and observance of the rights recognized in the present Covenant,

Agree upon the following articles:

Part 1

ARTICLE 1

1. All peoples have the right of self-determination. By virtue of that right they freely determine their political status and freely pursue their economic, social and cultural development.

2. All peoples may, for their own ends, freely dispose of their natural wealth and resources without prejudice to any obligations

arising out of international economic co-operation, based upon the principle of mutual benefit, and international law. In no case may a people be deprived of its own means of subsistence.

3. The States Parties to the present Covenant, including those having responsibility for the administration of Non-Self-Governing and Trust Territories, shall promote the realization of the right of self-determination, and shall respect that right, in conformity with the provisions of the Charter of the United Nations.

Part 2

ARTICLE 2

1. Each State Party to the present Covenant undertakes to respect and to ensure to all individuals within its territory and subject to its jurisdiction the rights recognized in the present Covenant, without distinction of any kind, such as race, colour, sex, language, religion, political or other opinion, national or social origin, property, birth or other status.

2. Where not already provided for by existing legislative or other measures, each State Party to the present Covenant undertakes to take the necessary steps, in accordance with its constitutional processes and with the provisions of the present Covenant, to adopt such legislative or other measures as may be necessary to give effect to the rights recognized in the present Covenant.

3. Each State Party to the present Covenant undertakes:

(*a*) To ensure that any person whose rights or freedoms as herein recognized are violated shall have an effective remedy, notwithstanding that the violation has been committed by persons acting in an official capacity;

(*b*) To ensure that any person claiming such a remedy shall have his right thereto determined by competent judicial, administrative or legislative authorities, or by any other competent authority provided for by the legal system of the State, and to develop the possibilities of judicial remedy;

(*c*) To ensure that the competent authorities shall enforce such remedies when granted.

ARTICLE 3

The States Parties to the present Covenant undertake to ensure the equal right of men and women to the enjoyment of all civil and political rights set forth in the present Covenant.

ARTICLE 4

1. In time of public emergency which threatens the life of the nation and the existence of which is officially proclaimed, the States Parties to the present Covenant may take measures derogating from their obligations under the present Covenant to the extent strictly required by the exigencies of the situation, provided that such measures are not inconsistent with their other obligations under international law and do not involve discrimination solely on the ground of race, colour, sex, language, religion or social origin.

2. No derogation from articles 6, 7, 8 (paragraphs 1 and 2), 11, 15, 16 and 18 may be made under this provision.

3. Any State Party to the present Covenant availing itself of the right of derogation shall immediately inform the other States Parties to the present Covenant, through the intermediary of the Secretary-General of the United Nations, of the provisions from which it has derogated and of the reasons by which it was actuated. A further communication shall be made, through the same intermediary, on the date on which it terminates such derogation.

ARTICLE 5

1. Nothing in the present Covenant may be interpreted as implying for any State, group or person any right to engage in any activity or perform any act aimed at the destruction of any of the rights and freedoms recognized herein or at their limitation to a greater extent than is provided for in the present Covenant.

2. There shall be no restriction upon or derogation from any of the fundamental human rights recognized or existing in any State Party to the present Covenant pursuant to law, conventions, regulations or custom on the pretext that the present Covenant does not recognize such rights or that it recognizes them to a lesser extent.

Part 3

ARTICLE 6

1. Every human being has the inherent right to life. This right shall be protected by law. No one shall be arbitrarily deprived of his life.

2. In countries which have not abolished the death penalty, sentence of death may be imposed only for the most serious crimes in accordance with the law in force at the time of the commission of the crime and not contrary to the provisions of the present Covenant and to the Convention on the Prevention and Punishment of the Crime of Genocide. This penalty can only be carried out pursuant to a final judgement rendered by a competent court.

3. When deprivation of life constitutes the crime of genocide, it is understood that nothing in this article shall authorize any State Party to the present Covenant to derogate in any way from any obligation assumed under the provisions of the Convention on the Prevention and Punishment of the Crime of Genocide.

4. Anyone sentenced to death shall have the right to seek pardon or commutation of the sentence. Amnesty, pardon or commutation of the sentence of death may be granted in all cases.

5. Sentence of death shall not be imposed for crimes committed by persons below eighteen years of age and shall not be carried out on pregnant women.

6. Nothing in this article shall be invoked to delay or to prevent the abolition of capital punishment by any State Party to the present Covenant.

ARTICLE 7

No one shall be subjected to torture or to cruel, inhuman or degrading treatment or punishment. In particular, no one shall be subjected without his free consent to medical or scientific experimentation.

ARTICLE 8

1. No one shall be held in slavery; slavery and the slave-trade in all their forms shall be prohibited.

2. No one shall be held in servitude.

3. (*a*) No one shall be required to perform forced or compulsory labour;

(*b*) Paragraph 3 (*a*) shall not be held to preclude, in countries where imprisonment with hard labour may be imposed as a punishment for a crime, the performance of hard labour in pursuance of a sentence to such punishment by a competent court;

(*c*) For the purpose of this paragraph the term "forced or compulsory labour" shall not include:

(i) Any work or service, not referred to in sub-paragraph (*b*), normally required of a person who is under detention in consequence of a lawful order of a court, or of a person during conditional release from such detention;

(ii) Any service of a military character and, in countries where conscientious objection is recognized, any national service required by law of conscientious objectors;

(iii) Any service exacted in cases of emergency or calamity threatening the life or well-being of the community;

(iv) Any work or service which forms part of normal civil obligations.

ARTICLE 9

1. Everyone has the right to liberty and security of person. No one shall be subjected to arbitrary arrest or detention. No one shall be deprived of his liberty except on such grounds and in accordance with such procedures as are established by law.

2. Anyone who is arrested shall be informed, at the time of arrest, of the reasons for his arrest and shall be promptly informed of any charges against him.

3. Anyone arrested or detained on a criminal charge shall be brought promptly before a judge or other officer authorized by law to exercise judicial power and shall be entitled to trial within a reasonable time or to release. It shall not be the general rule that persons awaiting trial shall be detained in custody, but release may be subject to guarantees to appear for trial, at any other stage of the judicial proceedings, and, should occasion arise, for execution of the judgement.

4. Anyone who is deprived of his liberty by arrest or detention shall

be entitled to take proceedings before a court, in order that that court may decide without delay on the lawfulness of his detention and order his release if the detention is not lawful.

5. Anyone who has been the victim of unlawful arrest or detention shall have an enforceable right to compensation.

ARTICLE 10

1. All persons deprived of their liberty shall be treated with humanity and with respect for the inherent dignity of the human person.

2. (*a*) Accused persons shall, save in exceptional circumstances, be segregated from convicted persons and shall be subject to separate treatment appropriate to their status as unconvicted persons;

(*b*) Accused juvenile persons shall be separated from adults and brought as speedily as possible for adjudication.

3. The penitentiary system shall comprise treatment of prisoners the essential aim of which shall be their reformation and social rehabilitation. Juvenile offenders shall be segregated from adults and be accorded treatment appropriate to their age and legal status.

ARTICLE 11

No one shall be imprisoned merely on the ground of inability to fulfill a contractual obligation.

ARTICLE 12

1. Everyone lawfully within the territory of a State shall, within that territory, have the right to liberty of movement and freedom to choose his residence.

2. Everyone shall be free to leave any country, including his own.

3. The above-mentioned rights shall not be subject to any restrictions except those which are provided by law, are necessary to protect national security, public order (*ordre public*), public health or morals or the rights and freedoms of others, and are consistent with the other rights recognized in the present Covenant.

4. No one shall be arbitrarily deprived of the right to enter his own country.

ARTICLE 13

An alien lawfully in the territory of a State Party to the present Covenant may be expelled therefrom only in pursuance of a decision reached in accordance with law and shall, except where compelling reasons of national security otherwise require, be allowed to submit the reasons against his expulsion and to have his case reviewed by, and be represented for the purpose before, the competent authority or a person or persons especially designated by the competent authority.

ARTICLE 14

1. All persons shall be equal before the courts and tribunals. In the determination of any criminal charge against him, or of his rights and obligations in a suit at law, everyone shall be entitled to a fair and public hearing by a competent, independent and impartial tribunal established by law. The Press and the public may be excluded from all or part of a trial for reasons of morals, public order (*ordre public*) or national security in a democratic society, or when the interest of the private lives of the parties so requires, or to the extent strictly necessary in the opinion of the court in special circumstances where publicity would prejudice the interests of justice; but any judgement rendered in a criminal case or in a suit at law shall be made public except where the interest of juvenile persons otherwise requires or the proceedings concern matrimonial disputes or the guardianship of children.

2. Everyone charged with a criminal offence shall have the right to be presumed innocent until proved guilty according to law.

3. In the determination of any criminal charge against him, everyone shall be entitled to the following minimum guarantees, in full equality:

(*a*) To be informed promptly and in detail in a language which he understands of the nature and cause of the charge against him;

(*b*) To have adequate time and facilities for the preparation of his defence and to communicate with counsel of his own choosing;

(*c*) To be tried without undue delay;

(*d*) To be tried in his presence, and to defend himself in person or through legal assistance of his own choosing; to be informed, if he does not have legal assistance, of this right; and to have legal assistance assigned to him, in any case where the interests of justice so require, and without payment by him in any such case if he does not have sufficient means to pay for it;

(*e*) To examine, or have examined, the witnesses against him and to obtain the attendance and examination of witnesses on his behalf under the same conditions as witnesses against him;

(*f*) To have the free assistance of an interpreter if he cannot understand or speak the language used in court;

(*g*) Not to be compelled to testify against himself or to confess guilt.

4. In the case of juvenile persons, the procedure shall be such as will take account of their age and the desirability of promoting their rehabilitation.

5. Everyone convicted of a crime shall have the right to his conviction and sentence being reviewed by a higher tribunal according to law.

6. When a person has by a final decision been convicted of a criminal offence and when subsequently his conviction has been reversed or he has been pardoned on the ground that a new or newly discovered fact shows conclusively that there has been a miscarriage of justice, the person who has suffered punishment as a result of such conviction shall be compensated according to law, unless it is proved that the non-disclosure of the unknown fact in time is wholly or partly attributable to him.

7. No one shall be liable to be tried or punished again for an offence for which he has already been finally convicted or acquitted in accordance with the law and penal procedure of each country.

ARTICLE 15

1. No one shall be held guilty of any criminal offence on account of any act or omission which did not constitute a criminal offence, under national or international law, at the time when it was committed. Nor shall a heavier penalty be imposed than the one that was applicable at the time when the criminal offence was committed. If, subsequent to the commission of the offence, provision is made by law for the imposition of a lighter penalty, the offender shall benefit thereby.

2. Nothing in this article shall prejudice the trial and punishment of any person for any act or omission which, at the time when it was committed, was criminal according to the general principles of law recognized by the community of nations.

ARTICLE 16

Everyone shall have the right to recognition everywhere as a person before the law.

ARTICLE 17

1. No one shall be subjected to arbitrary or unlawful interference with his privacy, family, home or correspondence, nor to unlawful attacks on his honour and reputation.

2. Everyone has the right to the protection of the law against such interference or attacks.

ARTICLE 18

1. Everyone shall have the right to freedom of thought, conscience and religion. This right shall include freedom to have or to adopt a religion or belief of his choice, and freedom, either individually or in community with others and in public or private, to manifest his religion or belief in worship, observance, practice and teaching.

2. No one shall be subject to coercion which would impair his freedom to have or to adopt a religion or belief of his choice.

3. Freedom to manifest one's religion or beliefs may be subject only to such limitations as are prescribed by law and are necessary to protect public safety, order, health, or morals or the fundamental rights and freedoms of others.

4. The States Parties to the present Covenant undertake to have respect for the liberty of parents and, when applicable, legal guardians to ensure the religious and moral education of their children in conformity with their own convictions.

ARTICLE 19

1. Everyone shall have the right to hold opinions without interference.

2. Everyone shall have the right to freedom of expression; this right shall include freedom to seek, receive and impart information and ideas of all kinds, regardless of frontiers, either orally, in writing or in print, in the form of art, or through any other media of his choice.

3. The exercise of the rights provided for in paragraph 2 of this article carries with it special duties and responsibilities. It may therefore be subject to certain restrictions, but these shall only be such as are provided by law and are necessary:

(*a*) For respect of the rights or reputations of others;

(*b*) For the protection of national security or of public order (*ordre public*), or of public health or morals.

ARTICLE 20

1. Any propaganda for war shall be prohibited by law.

2. Any advocacy of national, racial or religious hatred that constitutes incitement to discrimination, hostility or violence shall be prohibited by law.

ARTICLE 21

The right of peaceful assembly shall be recognized. No restrictions may be placed on the exercise of this right other than those imposed in conformity with the law and which are necessary in a democratic society in the interests of national security or public safety, public order (*ordre public*), the protection of public health or morals or the protection of the rights and freedoms of others.

ARTICLE 22

1. Everyone shall have the right to freedom of association with others, including the right to form and join trade unions for the protection of his interests.

2. No restrictions may be placed on the exercise of this right other than those which are prescribed by law and which are necessary in a democratic society in the interests of national security or public safety, public order (*ordre public*), the protection of public health or morals or the protection of the rights and freedoms of others. This article shall not prevent the imposition of lawful restrictions on

members of the armed forces and of the police in their exercise of this right.

3. Nothing in this article shall authorize States Parties to the International Labour Organisation Convention of 1948 concerning Freedom of Association and Protection of the Right to Organize to take legislative measures which would prejudice, or to apply the law in such a manner as to prejudice, the guarantees provided for in that Convention.

ARTICLE 23

1. The family is the natural and fundamental group unit of society and is entitled to protection by society and the State.

2. The right of men and women of marriageable age to marry and to found a family shall be recognized.

3. No marriage shall be entered into without the free and full consent of the intending spouses.

4. States Parties to the present Covenant shall take appropriate steps to ensure equality of rights and responsibilities of spouses as to marriage, during marriage and at its dissolution. In the case of dissolution, provision shall be made for the necessary protection of any children.

ARTICLE 24

1. Every child shall have, without any discrimination as to race, colour, sex, language, religion, national or social origin, property or birth, the right to such measures of protection as are required by his status as a minor, on the part of his family, society and the State.

2. Every child shall be registered immediately after birth and shall have a name.

3. Every child has the right to acquire a nationality.

ARTICLE 25

Every citizen shall have the right and the opportunity, without any of the distinctions mentioned in article 2 and without unreasonable restrictions:

(*a*) To take part in the conduct of public affairs, directly or through freely chosen representatives;

(*b*) To vote and to be elected at genuine periodic elections which shall be by universal and equal suffrage and shall be held by secret ballot, guaranteeing the free expression of the will of the electors;

(*c*) To have access, on general terms of quality, to public service in his country.

ARTICLE 26

All persons are equal before the law and are entitled without any discrimination to the equal protection of the law. In this respect, the law shall prohibit any discrimination and guarantee to all persons equal and effective protection against discrimination on any ground such as race, colour, sex, language, religion, political or other opinion, national or social origin, property, birth or other status.

ARTICLE 27

In those States in which ethnic, religious or linguistic minorities exist, persons belonging to such minorities shall not be denied the right, in community with the other members of their group, to enjoy their own culture, to profess and practise their own religion, or to use their own language.

Part 4

ARTICLE 28

1. There shall be established a Human Rights Committee (hereafter referred to in the present Covenant as the Committee). It shall consist of eighteen members and shall carry out the functions hereinafter provided.

2. The Committee shall be composed of nationals of the States Parties to the present Covenant who shall be persons of high moral character and recognized competence in the field of human rights, consideration being given to the usefulness of the participation of some persons having legal experience.

3. The members of the Committee shall be elected and shall serve in their personal capacity.

ARTICLE 29

1. The members of the Committee shall be elected by secret ballot from a list of persons possessing the qualifications prescribed in article 28 and nominated for the purpose by the States Parties to the present Covenant.

2. Each State Party to the present Covenant may nominate not more than two persons. These persons shall be nationals of the nominating State.

3. A person shall be eligible for renomination.

ARTICLE 30

1. The initial election shall be held no later than six months after the date of the entry into force of the present Covenant.

2. At least four months before the date of each election to the Committee other than an election to fill a vacancy declared in accordance with article 34, the Secretary-General of the United Nations shall address a written invitation to the States Parties to the present Covenant to submit their nominations for membership of the Committee within three months.

3. The Secretary-General of the United Nations shall prepare a list in alphabetical order of all the persons thus nominated, with an indication of the States Parties which have nominated them, and shall submit it to the States Parties to the present Covenant no later than one month before the date of each election.

4. Elections of the members of the Committee shall be held at a meeting of the States Parties to the present Covenant convened by the Secretary-General of the United Nations at the Headquarters of the United Nations. At that meeting, for which two-thirds of the States Parties to the present Covenant shall constitute a quorum, the persons elected to the Committee shall be those nominees who obtain the largest number of votes and an absolute majority of the votes of the representatives of States Parties present and voting.

ARTICLE 31

1. The Committee may not include more than one national of the same State.

2. In the election of the Committee, consideration shall be given to equitable geographical distribution of membership and to the representation of the different forms of civilization and of the principal legal systems.

ARTICLE 32

1. The members of the Committee shall be elected for a term of four years. They shall be eligible for re-election if renominated. However, the terms of nine of the members elected at the first election shall expire at the end of two years; immediately after the first election, the names of these nine members shall be chosen by lot by the Chairman of the meeting referred to in article 30, paragraph 4.

2. Elections at the expiry of office shall be held in accordance with the preceding articles of this part of the present Covenant.

ARTICLE 33

1. If, in the unanimous opinion of the other members, a member of the Committee has ceased to carry out his functions for any cause other than absence of a temporary character, the Chairman of the Committee shall notify the Secretary-General of the United Nations, who shall then declare the seat of that member to be vacant.

2. In the event of the death or the resignation of a member of the Committee, the Chairman shall immediately notify the Secretary-General of the United Nations, who shall declare the seat vacant from the date of death or the date on which the resignation takes effect.

ARTICLE 34

1. When a vacancy is declared in accordance with article 33 and if the term of office of the member to be replaced does not expire within six months of the declaration of the vacancy, the Secretary-General of the United Nations shall notify each of the States Parties to the

present Covenant, which may within two months submit nominations in accordance with article 29 for the purpose of filling the vacancy.

2. The Secretary-General of the United Nations shall prepare a list in alphabetical order of the persons thus nominated and shall submit it to the States Parties to the present Covenant. The election to fill the vacancy shall then take place in accordance with the relevant provisions of this part of the present Covenant.

3. A member of the Committee elected to fill a vacancy declared in accordance with article 33 shall hold office for the remainder of the term of the member who vacated the seat on the Committee under the provisions of that article.

ARTICLE 35

The members of the Committee shall, with the approval of the General Assembly of the United Nations, receive emoluments from United Nations resources on such terms and conditions as the General Assembly many decide, having regard to the importance of the Committee's responsibilities.

ARTICLE 36

The Secretary-General of the United Nations shall provide the necessary staff and facilities for the effective performance of the functions of the Committee under the present Covenant.

ARTICLE 37

1. The Secretary-General of the United Nations shall convene the initial meeting of the Committee at the Headquarters of the United Nations.

2. After its initial meeting, the Committee shall meet at such times as shall be provided in its rules of procedure.

3. The Committee shall normally meet at the Headquarters of the United Nations or at the United Nations Office at Geneva.

ARTICLE 38

Every member of the Committee shall, before taking up his duties, make a solemn declaration in open committee that he will perform his functions impartially and conscientiously.

ARTICLE 39

1. The Committee shall elect its officers for a term of two years. They may be re-elected.

2. The Committee shall establish its own rules of procedure, but these rules shall provide, *inter alia*, that:

(*a*) Twelve members shall constitute a quorum;

(*b*) Decisions of the Committee shall be made by a majority vote of the members present.

ARTICLE 40

1. The States Parties to the present Covenant undertake to submit reports on the measures they have adopted which give effect to the rights recognized herein and on the progress made in the enjoyment of those rights:

(*a*) Within one year of the entry into force of the present Covenant for the States Parties concerned;

(*b*) Thereafter whenever the Committee so requests.

2. All reports shall be submitted to the Secretary-General of the United Nations, who shall transmit them to the Committee for consideration. Reports shall indicate the factors and difficulties, if any, affecting the implementation of the present Covenant.

3. The Secretary-General of the United Nations may, after consultation with the Committee, transmit to the specialized agencies concerned copies of such parts of the reports as may fall within their field of competence.

4. The Committee shall study the reports submitted by the States Parties to the present Covenant. It shall transmit its reports, and such general comments as it may consider appropriate, to the States Parties. The Committee may also transmit to the Economic and Social Council these comments along with the copies of the reports it has received from States Parties to the present Covenant.

5. The States Parties to the present Covenant may submit to the Committee observations on any comments that may be made in accordance with paragraph 4 of this article.

ARTICLE 41

1. A State Party to the present Covenant may at any time declare under this article that it recognizes the competence of the Committee

to receive and consider communications to the effect that a State Party claims that another State Party is not fulfilling its obligations under the present Covenant. Communications under this article may be received and considered only if submitted by a State Party which has made a declaration recognizing in regard to itself the competence of the Committee. No communication shall be received by the Committee if it concerns a State Party which has not made such a declaration. Communications received under this article shall be dealt with in accordance with the following procedure:

(*a*) If a Party to the present Covenant considers that another State Party is not giving effect to the provisions of the present Covenant, it may, by written communication, bring the matter to the attention of that State Party. Within three months after the receipt of the communication, the receiving State shall afford the State which sent the communication an explanation or any other statement in writing clarifying the matter, which should include, to the extent possible and pertinent, reference to domestic procedures and remedies taken, pending, or available in the matter.

(*b*) If the matter is not adjusted to the satisfaction of both States Parties concerned within six months after the receipt by the receiving State of the initial communication, either State shall have the right to refer the matter to the Committee, by notice given to the Committee and to the other State.

(*c*) The Committee shall deal with a matter referred to it only after it has ascertained that all available domestic remedies have been invoked and exhausted in the matter, in conformity with the generally recognized principles of international law. This shall not be the rule where the application of the remedies is unreasonably prolonged.

(*d*) The Committee shall hold closed meetings when examining communications under this article.

(*e*) Subject to the provisions of sub-paragraph (*c*), the Committee shall make available its good offices to the States Parties concerned with a view to a friendly solution of the matter on the basis of respect for human rights and fundamental freedoms as recognized in the present Covenant.

(*f*) In any matter referred to it, the Committee may call upon the

States Parties concerned, referred to in sub-paragraph (*b*), to supply any relevant information.

(*g*) The States Parties concerned, referred to in sub-paragraph (*b*), shall have the right to be represented when the matter is being considered in the Committee and to make submissions orally and/or in writing.

(*h*) The Committee shall, within twelve months after the date of receipt of notice under sub-paragraph (*b*), submit a report:

(i) If a solution within the terms of sub-paragraph (*e*) is reached, the Committee shall confine its report to a brief statement of the facts and of the solution reached;

(ii) If a solution within the terms of sub-paragraph (*e*) is not reached, the Committee shall confine its report to a brief statement of the facts; the written submissions and record of the oral submissions made by the States Parties concerned shall be attached to the report.

In every matter, the report shall be communicated to the States Parties concerned.

2. The provisions of this article shall come into force when ten States Parties to the present Covenant have made declarations under paragraph 1 of this article. Such declarations shall be deposited by the States Parties with the Secretary-General of the United Nations, who shall transmit copies thereof to the other States Parties. A declaration may be withdrawn at any time by notification to the Secretary-General. Such a withdrawal shall not prejudice the consideration of any matter which is the subject of a communication already transmitted under this article; no further communication by any State Party shall be received after the notification of withdrawal of the declaration has been received by the Secretary-General, unless the State Party concerned had made a new declaration.

ARTICLE 42

1. (*a*) If a matter referred to the Committee in accordance with article 41 is not resolved to the satisfaction of the States Parties concerned, the Committee may, with the prior consent of the States Parties

concerned, appoint an *ad hoc* Conciliation Commission (hereinafter referred to as the Commission). The good offices of the Commission shall be made available to the States Parties concerned with a view to an amicable solution of the matter on the basis of respect for the present Covenant;

(*b*) The Commission shall consist of five persons acceptable to the States Parties concerned. If the States Parties concerned fail to reach agreement within three months on all or part of the composition of the Commission, the members of the Commission concerning whom no agreement has been reached shall be elected by secret ballot by a two-thirds majority vote of the Committee from among its members.

2. The members of the Commission shall serve in their personal capacity. They shall not be nationals of the States Parties concerned, or of a State not party to the present Covenant, or of a State Party which has not made a declaration under article 41.

3. The Commission shall elect its own Chairman and adopt its own rules of procedure.

4. The meetings of the Commission shall normally be held at the Headquarters of the United Nations or at the United Nations Office at Geneva. However, they may be held at such other convenient places as the Commission may determine in consultation with the Secretary-General of the United Nations and the States Parties concerned.

5. The secretariat provided in accordance with article 36 shall also service the commissions appointed under this article.

6. The information received and collated by the Committee shall be made available to the Commission and the Commission may call upon the States Parties concerned to supply any other relevant information.

7. When the Commission has fully considered the matter, but in any event not later than twelve months after having been seized of the matter, it shall submit to the Chairman of the Committee a report for communication to the States Parties concerned:

(*a*) If the Commission is unable to complete its consideration of the matter within twelve months, it shall confine its report to a brief statement of the status of its consideration of the matter;

(*b*) If an amicable solution to the matter on the basis of respect for human rights as recognized in the present Covenant is reached, the Commission shall confine its report to a brief statement of the facts and of the solution reached;

(c) If a solution within the terms of sub-paragraph (b) is not reached, the Commission's report shall embody its findings on all questions of fact relevant to the issues between the States Parties concerned, and its views on the possibilities of an amicable solution of the matter. This report shall also contain the written submissions and a record of the oral submissions made by the States Parties concerned;

(d) If the Commission's report is submitted under sub-paragraph (c), the States Parties concerned shall, within three months of the receipt of the report, notify the Chairman of the Committee whether or not they accept the contents of the report of the Commission.

8. The provisions of this article are without prejudice to the responsibilities of the Committee under article 41.

9. The States Parties concerned shall share equally all the expenses of the members of the Commission in accordance with estimates to be provided by the Secretary-General of the United Nations.

10. The Secretary-General of the United Nations shall be empowered to pay the expenses of the members of the Commission, if necessary, before reimbursement by the States Parties concerned, in accordance with paragraph 9 of this article.

ARTICLE 43

The members of the Committee, and of the *ad hoc* conciliation commissions which may be appointed under article 42, shall be entitled to the facilities, privileges and immunities of experts on mission for the United Nations as laid down in the relevant sections of the Convention on the Privileges and Immunities of the United Nations.

ARTICLE 44

The provisions for the implementation of the present Covenant shall apply without prejudice to the procedures prescribed in the field of human rights by or under the constituent instruments and the conventions of the United Nations and of the specialized agencies and shall not prevent the States Parties to the present Covenant from having recourse to other procedures for settling a dispute in accordance with general or special international agreements in force between them.

ARTICLE 45

The Committee shall submit to the General Assembly of the United Nations, through the Economic and Social Council, an annual report on its activities.

Part 5

ARTICLE 46

Nothing in the present Covenant shall be interpreted as impairing the provisions of the Charter of the United Nations and of the constitutions of the specialized agencies which define the respective responsibilities of the various organs of the United Nations and of the specialized agencies in regard to the matters dealt with in the present Covenant.

ARTICLE 47

Nothing in the present Covenant shall be interpreted as impairing the inherent right of all peoples to enjoy and utilize fully and freely their natural wealth and resources.

Part 6

ARTICLE 48

1. The present Covenant is open for signature by any State Member of the United Nations or member of any of its specialized agencies, by any State Party to the Statute of the International Court of Justice, and by any other State which has been invited by the General Assembly of the United Nations to become a party to the present Covenant.

2. The present Covenant is subject to ratification. Instruments of ratification shall be deposited with the Secretary-General of the United Nations.

3. The present Covenant shall be open to accession by any State referred to in paragraph 1 of this article.

4. Accession shall be effected by the deposit of an instrument of accession with the Secretary-General of the United Nations.

5. The Secretary-General of the United Nations shall inform all States which have signed this Covenant or acceded to it of the deposit of each instrument of ratification or accession.

ARTICLE 49

1. The present Covenant shall enter into force three months after the date of the deposit with the Secretary-General of the United Nations of the thirty-fifth instrument of ratification or instrument of accession.

2. For each State ratifying the present Covenant or acceding to it after the deposit of the thirty-fifth instrument of ratification or instrument of accession, the present Covenant shall enter into force three months after the date of the deposit of its own instrument of ratification or instrument of accession.

ARTICLE 50

The provisions of the present Covenant shall extend to all parts of federal States without any limitations or exceptions.

ARTICLE 51

1. Any State Party to the present Covenant may propose an amendment and file it with the Secretary-General of the United Nations. The Secretary-General of the United Nations shall thereupon communicate any proposed amendments to the States Parties to the present Covenant with a request that they notify him whether they favour a conference of States Parties for the purpose of considering and voting upon the proposals. In the event that at least one-third of the States Parties favours such a conference, the Secretary-General shall convene the conference under the auspices of the United Nations. Any amendment adopted by a majority of the States Parties present and voting at the conference shall be submitted to the General Assembly of the United Nations for approval.

2. Amendments shall come into force when they have been ap-

proved by the General Assembly of the United Nations and accepted by a two-thirds majority of the States Parties to the present Covenant in accordance with their respective constitutional processes.

3. When amendments come into force, they shall be binding on those States Parties which have accepted them, other States Parties still being bound by the provisions of the present Covenant and any earlier amendment which they have accepted.

ARTICLE 52

Irrespective of the notifications made under article 48, paragraph 5, the Secretary-General of the United Nations shall inform all States referred to in paragraph 1 of the same article of the following particulars:

(a) Signatures, ratifications and accessions under article 48;

(b) The date of the entry into force of the present Covenant under article 49 and the date of the entry into force of any amendments under article 51.

ARTICLE 53

1. The present Covenant, of which the Chinese, English, French, Russian and Spanish texts are equally authentic, shall be deposited in the archives of the United Nations.

2. The Secretary-General of the United Nations shall transmit certified copies of the present Covenant to all States referred to in article 48.

OPTIONAL PROTOCOL TO THE INTERNATIONAL COVENANT ON CIVIL AND POLITICAL RIGHTS

The States Parties to the present protocol,

Considering that in order further to achieve the purposes of the Covenant on Civil and Political Rights (hereinafter referred to as the Covenant) and the implementation of its provisions it would be appropriate to enable the Human Rights Committee set up in part IV of the Covenant (hereinafter referred to as the Committee) to receive and consider, as provided in the present Protocol, communications from individuals claiming to be victims of violations of any of the rights set forth in the Covenant,

Have agreed as follows:

ARTICLE 1

A State Party to the Covenant that becomes a party to the present Protocol recognizes the competence of the Committee to receive and consider communications from individuals subject to its jurisdiction who claim to be victims of a violation by that State Party of any of the rights set forth in the Covenant. No communication shall be received by the Committee if it concerns a State Party to the Covenant which is not a party to the present Protocol.

ARTICLE 2

Subject to the provisions of article 1, individuals who claim that any of their rights enumerated in the Covenant have been violated and who have exhausted all available domestic remedies may submit a written communication to the Committee for consideration.

ARTICLE 3

The Committee shall consider inadmissible any communication under the present Protocol which is anonymous, or which it considers to be an abuse of the rights of submission of such communications or to be incompatible with the provisions of the Covenant.

ARTICLE 4

1. Subject to the provisions of article 3, the Committee shall bring any communications submitted to it under the present Protocol to the attention of the State Party to the present Protocol alleged to be violating any provisions of the Covenant.

2. Within six months, the receiving State shall submit to the Committee written explanations or statements clarifying the matter and the remedy, if any, that may have been taken by that State.

ARTICLE 5

1. The Committee shall consider communications received under the present Protocol in the light of all written information made available to it by the individual and by the State Party concerned.

2. The Committee shall not consider any communication from an individual unless it has ascertained that:

(*a*) The same matter is not being examined under another procedure of international investigation or settlement;

(*b*) The individual has exhausted all available domestic remedies. This shall not be the rule where the application of the remedies is unreasonably prolonged.

3. The Committee shall hold closed meetings when examining communications under the present Protocol.

4. The Committee shall forward its views to the State Party concerned and to the individual.

ARTICLE 6

The Committee shall include in its annual report under article 45 of the Covenant a summary of its activities under the present Protocol.

ARTICLE 7

Pending the achievement of the objectives of resolution 1514 (XV) adopted by the General Assembly of the United Nations on 14

December 1960 concerning the Declaration on the Granting of Independence to Colonial Countries and Peoples, the provisions of the present Protocol shall in no way limit the right of petition granted to these peoples by the Charter of the United Nations and other international conventions and instruments under the United Nations and its specialized agencies.

ARTICLE 8

1. The present Protocol is open for signature by any State which has signed the Covenant.

2. The present Protocol is subject to ratification by any State which has ratified or acceded to the Covenant. Instruments of ratification shall be deposited with the Secretary-General of the United Nations.

3. The present Protocol shall be open to accession by any State which has ratified or acceded to the Covenant.

4. Accession shall be effected by the deposit of an instrument of accession with the Secretary-General of the United Nations.

5. The Secretary-General of the United Nations shall inform all States which have signed the present Protocol or acceded to it of the deposit of each instrument of ratification or accession.

ARTICLE 9

1. Subject to the entry into force of the Covenant, the present Protocol shall enter into force three months after the date of the deposit with the Secretary-General of the United Nations of the tenth instrument of ratification or instrument of accession.

2. For each State ratifying the present Protocol or acceding to it after the deposit of the tenth instrument of ratification or instrument of accession, the present Protocol shall enter into force three months after the date of the deposit of its own instrument of ratification or instrument of accession.

ARTICLE 10

The provisions of the present Protocol shall extend to all parts of federal States without any limitations or exceptions.

ARTICLE 11

1. Any State Party to the present Protocol may propose an amendment and file it with the Secretary-General of the United Nations. The Secretary-General shall thereupon communicate any proposed amendments to the States Parties to the present Protocol with a request that they notify him whether they favour a conference of States Parties for the purpose of considering and voting upon the proposal. In the event that at least one-third of the States Parties favours such a conference, the Secretary-General shall convene the conference under the auspices of the United Nations. Any amendment adopted by a majority of the States Parties present and voting at the conference shall be submitted to the General Assembly of the United Nations for approval.

2. Amendments shall come into force when they have been approved by the General Assembly of the United Nations and accepted by a two-thirds majority of the States Parties to the present Protocol in accordance with their respective constitutional processes.

3. When amendments come into force, they shall be binding on those States Parties which have accepted them, other States Parties still being bound by the provisions of the present Protocol and any earlier amendment which they have accepted.

ARTICLE 12

1. Any State Party may denounce the present Protocol at any time by written notification addressed to the Secretary-General of the United Nations. Denunciation shall take effect three months after the date of receipt of the notification by the Secretary-General.

2. Denunciation shall be without prejudice to the continued application of the provisions of the present Protocol to any communication submitted under article 2 before the effective date of denunciation.

ARTICLE 13

Irrespective of the notifications made under article 8, paragraph 5, of the present Protocol, the Secretary-General of the United Nations shall inform all States referred to in article 48, paragraph 1, of the Covenant of the following particulars:

(a) Signatures, ratifications and accessions under article 8;

(*b*) The date of the entry into force of the present Protocol under article 9 and the date of the entry into force of any amendments under article 11;

(*c*) Denunciations under article 12.

ARTICLE 14

1. The present Protocol, of which the Chinese, English, French, Russian and Spanish texts are equally authentic, shall be deposited in the archives of the United Nations.

2. The Secretary-General of the United Nations shall transmit certified copies of the present Protocol to all States referred to in article 48 of the Covenant.

THE UNITED NATIONS DECLARATION ON THE ELIMINATION OF DISCRIMINATION AGAINST WOMEN

The Declaration

PREAMBLE

The Preamble to the Declaration sets forth the underlying convictions and concerns of the United Nations in regard to discrimination against women:

The General Assembly

Considering that the peoples of the United Nations have, in the Charter reaffirmed their faith in fundamental human rights, in the dignity and worth of the human person and in the equal rights of men and women,

Considering that the Universal Declaration of Human Rights asserts the principle of non-discrimination and proclaims that all human beings are born free and equal in dignity and rights and that everyone is entitled to all the rights and freedoms set forth therein, without distinction of any kind, including any distinction as to sex,

Taking into account the resolutions, declarations, conventions and recommendations of the United Nations and the specialized agencies designed to eliminate all forms of discrimination and to promote equal rights for men and women,

Concerned that, despite the Charter of the United Nations, the Universal Declaration of Human Rights, the International Covenants on Human Rights and other instruments of the United Nations and the specialized agencies and despite the progress made in the matter of equality of rights, there continues to exist considerable discrimination against women,

Considering that discrimination against women is incompatible with human dignity and with the welfare of the family and of society, prevents their participation, on equal terms with men, in the political, social, economic and cultural life of their countries and is an obstacle to the full development of the potentialities of women in the service of their countries and of humanity,

Bearing in mind the great contribution made by women to social, political, economic and cultural life and the part they play in the family and particularly in the rearing of children,

Convinced that the full and complete development of a country, the welfare of the world and the cause of peace require the maximum participation of women as well as men in all fields,

Considering that it is necessary to ensure the universal recognition in law and in fact of the principle of equality of men and women,

Solemnly proclaims this Declaration . . . .

The Preamble emphasizes not only that discrimination against women is unjust, and "incompatible with human dignity and with the welfare of the family and of society," but that women's full services and talents are needed, alongside those of men, for "the full and complete development of a country, the welfare of the world and the cause of peace." The Assembly proclaims the Declaration "to ensure the universal recognition in law and in fact of the principle of equality of men and women."

ARTICLE 1

Discrimination against women, denying or limiting as it does their equality of rights with men, is fundamentally unjust and constitutes an offence against human dignity.

ARTICLE 2

All appropriate measures shall be taken to abolish existing laws, customs, regulations and practices which are discriminatory against women, and to establish adequate legal protection for equal rights of men and women; in particular:

(*a*) The principle of equality of rights shall be embodied in the constitution or otherwise guaranteed by law;

(*b*) The international instruments of the United Nations and the specialized agencies relating to the elimination of discrimination against women shall be ratified or acceded to and fully implemented as soon as practicable.

ARTICLE 3

All appropriate measures shall be taken to educate public opinion and to direct national aspirations towards the eradication of prejudice and the abolition of customary and all other practices which are based on the idea of the inferiority of women.

ARTICLE 4

All appropriate measures shall be taken to ensure to women on equal terms with men, without any discrimination:

(*a*) The right to vote in all elections and be eligible for election to all publicly-elected bodies;

(*b*) The right to vote in all public referenda;

(*c*) The right to hold public office and to exercise all public functions. Such rights shall be guaranteed by legislation.

ARTICLE 5

Women shall have the same rights as men to acquire, change or retain their nationality. Marriage to an alien shall not automatically affect the nationality of the wife either by rendering her stateless or by forcing upon her the nationality of her husband.

ARTICLE 6

1. Without prejudice to the safeguarding of the unity and the harmony of the family, which remains the basic unit of any society, all appropriate measures, particularly legislative measures, shall be taken to ensure to women, married or unmarried, equal rights with men in the field of civil law, and in particular:

(*a*) The right to acquire, administer, enjoy, dispose of and inherit property, including property acquired during marriage;

(*b*) The right to equality in legal capacity and the exercise thereof;

(*c*) The same rights as men with regard to the law on the movement of persons.

2. All appropriate measures shall be taken to ensure the principle of equality of status of the husband and wife, and in particular:

(*a*) Women shall have the same right as men to free choice of a spouse and to enter into marriage only with their free and full consent;

(*b*) Women shall have equal rights with men during marriage and at its dissolution. In all cases the interest of the children shall be paramount;

(*c*) Parents shall have equal rights and duties in matters relating to their children. In all cases the interest of the children shall be paramount.

3. Child marriage and the betrothal of young girls before puberty shall be prohibited, and effective action, including legislation, shall be taken to specify a minimum age for marriage and to make the registration of marriages in an official registry compulsory.

ARTICLE 7

All provisions of penal codes which constitute discrimination against women shall be repealed.

ARTICLE 8

All appropriate measures, including legislation, shall be taken to combat all form of traffic in women and exploitation of prostitution of women.

ARTICLE 9

All appropriate measures shall be taken to ensure to girls and women, married or unmarried, equal rights with men in education at all levels, and in particular:

(*a*) Equal conditions of access to, and study in, educational institutions of all types, including universities and vocational, technical and professional schools;

(*b*) The same choice of curricula, the same examinations, teaching staff with qualifications of the same standard, and school premises and equipment of the same quality, whether the institutions are co-educational or not;

(*c*) Equal opportunities to benefit from scholarships and other study grants;

(*d*) Equal opportunities for access to programmes of continuing education, including adult literacy programmes;

(*e*) Access to educational information to help in ensuring the health and well-being of families.

ARTICLE 10

1. All appropriate measures shall be taken to ensure to women, married or unmarried, equal rights with men in the field of economic and social life, and in particular:

(*a*) The right, without discrimination on grounds of marital status or any other grounds, to receive vocational training, to work, to free choice of profession and employment, and to professional and vocational advancement;

(*b*) The right to equal remuneration with men and to equality of treatment in respect of work of equal value;

(*c*) The right to leave with pay, retirement privileges and provision for security in respect of unemployment, sickness, old age or other incapacity to work;

(*d*) The right to receive family allowances on equal terms with men.

2. In order to prevent discrimination against women on account of marriage or maternity and to ensure their effective right to work, measures shall be taken to prevent their dismissal in the event of marriage or maternity and to provide paid maternity leave, with the guarantee of returning to former employment, and to provide the necessary social services, including child-care facilities.

3. Measures taken to protect women in certain types of work, for reasons inherent in their physical nature, shall not be regarded as discriminatory.

ARTICLE 11

1. The principle of equality of rights of men and women demands implementation in all States in accordance with the principles of the Charter of the United Nations and of the Universal Declaration of Human Rights.

2. Governments, non-governmental organizations and individuals are urged, therefore, to do all in their power to promote the implementation of the principles contained in this Declaration.

THE HELSINKI AGREEMENT

*Principle VII (guiding relations between Participating
States) Respect for Human Rights and
Fundamental Freedoms, Including the Freedom of Thought,
Conscience, Religion, or Belief*

The participating States will respect human rights and fundamental freedoms, including the freedom of thought, conscience, religion or belief, for all without distinction as to race, sex, language or religion.

They will promote and encourage the effective exercise of civil, political, economic, social, cultural and other rights and freedoms all of which derive from the inherent dignity of the human person and are essential for his free and full development.

Within this framework the participating States will recognize and respect the freedom of the individual to profess and practise, alone or in community with others, religion or belief acting in accordance with the dictates of his own conscience.

The participating States on whose territory national minorities exist will respect the right of persons belonging to such minorities to equality before the law, will afford them the full opportunity for the actual enjoyment of human rights and fundamental freedoms and will, in this manner, protect their legitimate interests in this sphere.

The participating States recognize the universal significance of human rights and fundamental freedoms, respect for which is an essential factor for the peace, justice and well-being necessary to ensure the development of friendly relations and co-operation among themselves as among all States.

They will constantly respect these rights and freedoms in their mutual relations and will endeavour jointly and separately, including in co-operation with the United Nations, to promote universal and effective respect for them.

They confirm the right of the individual to know and act upon his rights and duties in this field.

In the field of human rights and fundamental freedoms, the participating States will act in conformity with the purposes and principles of the Charter of the United Nations and with the Universal Declaration of Human Rights. They will also fulfill their obligations as set forth in the international declarations and agreements in this field, including inter alia the International Covenants on Human Rights, by which they may be bound.

Co-operation in Humanitarian and Other Fields

The participating States:

Desiring to contribute to the strengthening of peace and understanding among peoples and to the spiritual enrichment of the human personality without distinction as to race, sex, language or religion,

Conscious that increased cultural and educational exchanges, broader dissemination of information, contacts between people, and the solution of humanitarian problems will contribute to the attainment of these aims,

Determined therefore to co-operate among themselves, irrespective of their political, economic and social systems, in order to create better conditions in the above fields, to develop and strengthen existing forms of co-operation and to work out new ways and means appropriate to these aims,

Convinced that this co-operation should take place in full respect for the principles guiding relations among participating States as set forth in the relevant document,

Have adopted the following:

1. HUMAN CONTACTS

The participating States:

Considering the development of contacts to be an important element in the strengthening of friendly relations and trust among peoples,

Affirming, in relation to their present effort to improve conditions in this area, the importance they attach to humanitarian considerations,

Desiring in this spirit to develop, with the continuance of détente, further efforts to achieve continuing progress in this field,

And conscious that the question relevant hereto must be settled by the States concerned under mutually acceptable conditions,

Make it their aim to facilitate freer movement and contacts, individually and collectively, whether privately or officially, among persons, institutions and organizations of the participating States, and to contribute to the solution of the humanitarian problems that arise in that connexion,

Declare their readiness to these ends to take measures which they consider appropriate and to conclude agreements or arrangements among themselves, as may be needed, and

Express their intention now to proceed to the implementation of the following:

(a) Contacts and Regular Meetings on the Basis of Family Ties

In order to promote further development of contacts on the basis of family ties the participating States will favourably consider applications for travel with the purpose of allowing persons to enter or leave their territory temporarily, and on a regular basis if desired, in order to visit members of their families.

Applications for temporary visits to meet members of their families will be dealt with without distinction as to the country of origin or destination: existing requirements for travel documents and visas will be applied in that spirit. The preparation and issue of such documents and visas will be effected within reasonable time limits; cases of urgent necessity—such as serious illness or death—will be given priority treatment. They will take such steps as may be necessary to ensure that the fees for official travel documents and visas are acceptable.

They confirm that the presentation of an application concerning contacts on the basis of family ties will not modify the rights and obligations of the applicant or of members of his family.

(b) Reunification of Families

The participating States will deal in a positive and humanitarian spirit with the applications of persons who wish to be reunited with members of their family, with special attention being given to requests of an urgent character—such as requests submitted by persons who are ill or old.

They will deal with applications in this field as expeditiously as possible.

They will lower where necessary the fees charged in connexion with these applications to ensure that they are at a moderate level.

Applications for the purpose of family reunification which are not granted may be renewed at the appropriate level and will be reconsidered at reasonably short intervals by the authorities of the country of residence or destination, whichever is concerned; under such circumstances fees will be charged only when applications are granted.

Persons whose applications for family reunification are granted may bring with them or ship their household and personal effects; to this end the participating States will use all possibilities provided by existing regulations.

Until members of the same family are reunited meetings and contacts between them may take place in accordance with the modalities for contacts on the basis of family ties.

The participating States will support the efforts of Red Cross and Red Crescent Societies concerned with the problems of family reunification.

They confirm that the presentation of an application concerning family reunification will not modify the rights and obligations of the applicant or of members of his family.

The receiving participating State will take appropriate care with regard to employment for persons from other participating States who take up permanent residence in that State in connexion with family reunification with its citizens and see that they are afforded opportunities equal to those enjoyed by its own citizens for education, medical assistance and social security.

(c) Marriage between Citizens of Different States

The participating States will examine favourably and on the basis of humanitarian considerations requests for exit or entry permits from persons who have decided to marry a citizen from another participating State.

The processing and issuing of the documents required for the above purposes and for the marriage will be in accordance with the provisions accepted for family reunification.

In dealing with requests from couples from different participating States, once married, to enable them and the minor children of their marriage to transfer their permanent residence to a State in which either one is normally a resident, the participating States will also apply the provisions accepted for family reunification.

(d) Travel for Personal or Professional Reasons

The participating States intend to facilitate wider travel by their citizens for personal or professional reasons and to this end they intend in particular:

—gradually to simplify and to administer flexibly the procedures for exit and entry;

—to ease regulations concerning movement of citizens from the other participating States in their territory, with due regard to security requirements.

They will endeavour gradually to lower, where necessary, the fees for visas and official travel documents.

They intend to consider, as necessary, means—including insofar as appropriate, the conclusion of multilateral or bilateral consular conventions or other relevant agreements or understandings—for the improvement of arrangements to provide consular services, including legal and consular assistance.

They confirm that religious faiths, institutions and organizations, practising within the constitutional framework of the participating States, and their representatives can, in the field of their activities, have contacts and meetings among themselves and exchange information.

These excerpts are from the final act of the Conference on Security and Cooperation in Europe. The Agreement was signed on August 1, 1975, in Helsinki by thirty-three European states, the U.S.A. and Canada.

DECLARATION ON THE PROTECTION OF ALL PERSONS FROM TORTURE AND OTHER CRUEL, INHUMAN OR DEGRADING TREATMENT OR PUNISHMENT

Adopted unanimously by United Nations General Assembly resolution 3452 (XXX) of 9 December 1975

ARTICLE 1

1. For the purpose of this Declaration, torture means any act by which severe pain or suffering, whether physical or mental, is intentionally inflicted by or at the instigation of a public official on a person for such purposes as obtaining from him or a third person information or confession, punishing him for an act he has committed or is suspected of having committed, or intimidating him or other persons. It does not include pain or suffering arising only from, inherent in or incidental to, lawful sanctions to the extent consistent with the Standard Minimum Rules for the Treatment of Prisoners.

2. Torture constitutes an aggravated and deliberate form of cruel, inhuman or degrading treatment or punishment.

ARTICLE 2

Any act of torture or other cruel, inhuman or degrading treatment or punishment is an offence to human dignity and shall be condemned as a denial of the purposes of the Charter of the United Nations and as a violation of the human rights and fundamental freedoms proclaimed in the Universal Declaration of Human Rights.

ARTICLE 3

No state may permit or tolerate torture or other cruel, inhuman or degrading treatment or punishment. Exceptional circumstances such as a state of war or a threat of war, internal political instability or any other public emergency may not be invoked as a justification of torture or other cruel, inhuman or degrading treatment or punishment.

ARTICLE 4

Each State shall, in accordance with the provisions of this Declaration, take effective measures to prevent torture and other cruel, inhuman or degrading treatment or punishment from being practised within its jurisdiction.

ARTICLE 5

The training of law enforcement personnel and of other public officials who may be responsible for persons deprived of their liberty shall ensure that full account is taken of the prohibition against torture and other cruel, inhuman or degrading treatment or punishment. This prohibition shall also, where appropriate, be included in such general rules or instructions as are issued in regard to the duties and functions of anyone who may be involved in the custody or treatment of such persons.

ARTICLE 6

Each State shall keep under systematic review interrogation methods and practices as well as arrangements for the custody and treatment of persons deprived of their liberty in its territory, with a view to preventing any cases of torture or other cruel, inhuman or degrading treatment or punishment.

ARTICLE 7

Each State shall ensure that all acts of torture as defined in article 1 are offences under its criminal law. The same shall apply in regard to acts which constitute participation in, complicity in, incitement to or an attempt to commit torture.

ARTICLE 8

Any person who alleges that he has been subjected to torture or other cruel, inhuman or degrading treatment or punishment by or at the instigation of a public official shall have the right to complain to, and to have his case impartially examined by, the competent authorities of the State concerned.

ARTICLE 9

Wherever there is reasonable ground to believe that an act of torture as defined in article 1 has been committed, the competent authorities of the State concerned shall promptly proceed to an impartial investigation even if there has been no formal complaint.

ARTICLE 10

If an investigation under article 8 or article 9 establishes that an act of torture as defined in article 1 appears to have been committed, criminal proceedings shall be instituted against the alleged offender or offenders in accordance with national law. If an allegation of cruel, inhuman or degrading treatment or punishment is considered to be well founded, the alleged offender or offenders shall be subject to criminal, disciplinary or other appropriate proceedings.

ARTICLE 11

Where it is proved that an act of torture or other cruel, inhuman or degrading treatment or punishment has been committed by or at the instigation of a public official, the victim shall be afforded redress and compensation in accordance with national law.

ARTICLE 12

Any statement which is established to have been made as a result of torture or other cruel, inhuman or degrading treatment may not be invoked as evidence against the person concerned or against any other person in any proceedings.

INTERNATIONAL INSTRUMENTS RELATED TO HUMAN RIGHTS IN CHRONOLOGICAL ORDER OF ADOPTION

DATE OF
ADOPTION   INSTRUMENT

1945
>June 26 Charter of United Nations

1948
>July 9 Freedom of Association and Protection of the Right to Organise Convention (I.L.O.)
>
>December 9 Convention on the Prevention and Punishment of the Crime of Genocide
>
>December 10 Universal Declaration of Human Rights

1949
>July 1 Right to Organise and Collective Bargaining Convention (I.L.O.)
>
>August 12 The Geneva Conventions of 1949
>
>December 2 Convention for the Suppression of the Traffic in Persons and of the Exploitation of the Prostitution of Others

1950
>December 14 Statute of the Office of the United Nations High Commissioner for Refugees

1951
>June 29 Equal Remuneration Convention (I.L.O.)
>
>July 28 Convention relating to the Status of Refugees

December 3   Convention concerning the International Exchange
               of Publications (U.N.E.S.C.O.)
December 3   Convention concerning the Exchange of Official
               Publications and Government Documents be-
               tween States (U.N.E.S.C.O.)

1959
November 20   Declaration of the Rights of the Child

1960
December 14   Convention against Discrimination in Education
               (U.N.E.S.C.O.)
December 14   Declaration on the Granting of Independence to
               Colonial Countries and Peoples

1961
August 30   Convention on the Reduction of Statelessness
October 26   International Convention for the Protection of Per-
               formers, Producers of Phonograms and Broad-
               casting Organizations (U.N.E.S.C.O.)

1962
November 7   Convention on Consent to Marriage, Minimum Age
               for Marriage and Registration of Marriages
December 10   Protocol Instituting a Conciliation and Good Offices
               Commission to be responsible for seeking a settle-
               ment of any disputes which may arise between
               States Parties to the Convention against Discrimi-
               nation in Education (U.N.E.S.C.O.)
December 14   General Assembly resolution 1803 (XVII) of 14
               December 1962, "Permanent Sovereignty over
               Natural Resources"

1963
November 20   United Nations Declaration on the Elimination of
               All Forms of Racial Discrimination

DATE OF ADOPTION	INSTRUMENT
1964	
July 9	Employment Policy Convention (I.L.O.)
1965	
November 1	Recommendation on Consent to Marriage, Minimum Age for Marriage and Registration of Marriages
December 7	Declaration on the Promotion among Youth of the Ideals of Peace, Mutual Respect and Understanding between Peoples
December 21	International Convention on the Elimination of All Forms of Racial Discrimination
1966	
November 4	Declaration of the Principles of International Cultural Co-operation
December 16	International Covenant on Economic, Social and Cultural Rights
December 16	International Covenant on Civil and Political Rights
December 16	Optional Protocol to the International Covenant on Civil and Political Rights
December 16	Protocol relating to the Status of Refugees
1967	
November 7	Declaration on the Elimination of Discrimination against Women
December 14	Declaration on Territorial Asylum
1968	
May 13	Proclamation of Teheran
November 26	Convention on the Non-Applicability of Statutory Limitations to War Crimes and Crimes against Humanity
1969	
December 11	Declaration on Social Progress and Development

DATE OF
ADOPTION   INSTRUMENT

1970

October 24 — International Development Strategy for the Second Development Decade

November 14 — Convention on the Means of Prohibiting and Preventing the Illicit Import, Export and Transfer of Ownership of Cultural Property (U.N.E.S.C.O.)

December 15 — Programme of Concerted International Action for the Advancement of Women

1971

June 23 — Workers' Representatives Convention (I.L.O.)

July 24 — Universal Copyright Convention as revised at Paris on 24 July 1971 (U.N.E.S.C.O.) Protocol Nos. 1-2 to the Universal Copyright Convention as revised at Paris on 24 July 1971 (U.N.E.S.C.O.)

October 29 — Convention for the Protection of Producers of Phonograms against Unauthorized Duplication of their Phonograms (U.N.E.S.C.O.)

November 16 — Convention concerning the Protection of the World Cultural and Natural Heritage (U.N.E.S.C.O.)

December 20 — Declaration on the Rights of Mentally Retarded Persons

1973

June 23 — Minimum Age Convention (I.L.O.)

November 30 — International Convention on the Suppression and Punishment of the Crime of Apartheid

1974

May 1 — Declaration and Programme of Action on the Establishment of a New Economic Order

May 21 — Convention relating to the Distribution of Programme-carrying Signals Transmitted by Satellite (U.N.E.S.C.O.)

June 24 — Paid Educational Leave Convention (I.L.O.)

DATE OF ADOPTION	INSTRUMENT
August 30	World Population Plan of Action
November 16	Universal Declaration on the Eradication of Hunger and Malnutrition
December 12	Charter of Economic Rights and Duties of States

1975

June 23	Rural Workers' Organizations Convention (I.L.O.)
June 24	Migrant Workers Convention (I.L.O.)
June 25	Declaration on Equality of Opportunity and Treatment for Women Workers (I.L.O.)
July 1	World Plan of Action for the Implementation of the Objectives of the International Women's Year
July 2	Declaration of Mexico on the Equality of Women and their Contribution to Development and Peace
November 10	Declaration on the Use of Scientific and Technological Progress in the Interests of Peace and for the Benefit of Mankind
December 9	Declaration on the Rights of Disabled Persons
December 9	Declaration on the Protection of All Persons from Being Subjected to Torture and Other Cruel, Inhuman or Degrading Treatment or Punishment

1976

June	Seafarers Annual Leave With Pay Convention (I.L.O.)

1977

June	Convention Concerning the Protection of Workers Against Occupational Hazards in the Working Environment due to Air Pollution, Noise and Vibration (I.L.O.)
June	Convention on the Employment and Conditions of Work and Life of Nursing Personnel (I.L.O.)

REGIONAL INSTRUMENTS RELATED TO HUMAN RIGHTS IN CHRONOLOGICAL ORDER OF ADOPTION

DATE OF ADOPTION	INSTRUMENT
1948	
May 2	American Declaration of the Rights and Duties of Man
1950	
November 4	[European] Convention for the Protection of Human Rights and Fundamental Freedoms
1952	
March 20	Protocol No. 1 to the European Convention
1959	
September 18	Rules of the Court of the European Court of Human Rights
1960	
June 8	Statute of the Inter-American Commission on Human Rights
1963	
May 6	Protocol No. 2 to the European Convention
May 6	Protocol No. 3 to the European Convention
September 16	Protocol No. 4 to the European Convention
1966	
January 20	Protocol No. 5 to the European Convention
1969	
November 22	American Convention on Human Rights
1974	
July 19	Regional Convention on the Recognition of Studies, Diplomas and Degrees in Higher Education in Latin America and the Caribbean (U.N.E.S.C.O.)

Index